DATA SCIENCE FOR SOCIAL GOOD

Ogbeide Sylvanus Uwagboe

Copyright © 2021
Ogbeide Sylvanus Uwagboe

Published In Nigeria by:
Emphaloz Publishing House
www.emphaloz.com

All rights reserved.

No part of this book may be reproduced, distributed, or transmitted in any form or by any means, including photocopying, or other electronic or mechanical methods, without the prior written permission of the publisher, except in the case of brief quotations embodied in critical reviews and certain non-commercial uses permitted by copyright law

TABLE OF CONTENT

Dedication iv
Preface v
Foreword vi
Introduction... viii

Chapter 1
   Understanding the Mission of Data for Social Good 1

Chapter 2
   Foundations of Data Science in the Public Sphere 9

Chapter 3
   Identifying Problems Worth Solving 18

Chapter 4
   Data Collection in Low-Resource Environments 27

Chapter 5
   Cleaning Structuring and Humanizing Data 37

Chapter 6
   Designing Solutions that Serve the Marginalized................................... 47

Chapter 7
   Case Studies from the Global South 57

Chapter 8
   The Politics of Data: Power Privacy and Policy 68

Chapter 9
   Measuring What Matters.. 77

Chapter 10
   Building a Career or Movement in Data for Good 88

DEDICATION

To the communities whose stories are often hidden in the margins of spreadsheets and to the data scientists, researchers, and changemakers who believe that numbers should serve justice, equity, and dignity.

This book is for you.

PREFACE

The idea for this book was born out of a deep concern: while data science continues to revolutionize industries, its impact on underserved communities often lags behind. Much of the world's innovation is measured in profit margins, but this book is grounded in a different metric human dignity.

Data Science for Social Good is not about showcasing the most complex algorithms or the flashiest tools. It's about exploring how data, when applied thoughtfully, can solve pressing social problems, inform public policy, and uplift lives at scale. The goal is not to impress, but to equip to offer frameworks, examples, and reflections that bridge the gap between technical know-how and real-world impact.

As a discipline, data science is only as powerful as the values that guide it. In these pages, you'll find stories from across the globe, lessons from lived experience, and methods shaped not only by logic but by empathy. This book is for data professionals seeking meaning, for nonprofits navigating technology, and for students who want to make a difference but don't know where to begin.

If you believe data should be more than a business asset if you believe it should be a tool for justice, then you are holding the right book.

FOREWORD

In recent years, the term "data science" has gained prominence across sectors from healthcare and education to finance and entertainment. Yet, despite its transformative potential, the role of data in advancing social goods remains underexplored, underfunded, and often misunderstood.

Data Science for Social Good arrives at a critical moment. It bridges the widening gap between those with the technical power to shape the future, and the communities who most urgently need that future to be more equitable. It challenges us to think differently not only about what we build, but who we build it for.

This book is not just an academic exercise or a call for better models. It is a call for moral imagination. It urges us to move beyond dashboards and datasets, to see the lives behind the numbers, and to center justice as a design principle in every solution we create.

The stories and lessons in this book are rooted in practical experience, but their impact is philosophical. They remind us that true innovation is not defined by speed or efficiency, but by empathy and accountability. If you are a data scientist, a policy leader, a student, or a social sector worker looking to use data meaningfully, this book is both a compass and a call to action.

Read it with an open mind, use it with bold conviction, and pass it on to the next generation of thinkers who believe that data should serve people not the other way around.

By Dr. Alima Okonkwo,

Public Interest Technologist and Founder, Data For Change Africa.

INTRODUCTION

The age of data is here. We track our steps, monitor our health, measure our performance, and analyze behaviors on a global scale. Algorithms now shape what we see, how we vote, what we buy, and even how justice is served. But as data-driven tools become more powerful, a critical question arises: powerful for whom?

Data Science for Social Good is not another guide to coding or machine learning. It is a reflection on how we wield data when the stakes involve people's lives do not profit. It explores what happens when we shift our focus from optimizing convenience to advancing equity. It invites us to think critically about the systems we build, and the voices we amplify or exclude in the process.

This book speaks to a diverse audience. It is for the data scientist searching for meaningful work, the nonprofit worker wondering how to turn data into action, the policymaker navigating digital transformation, and the student who believes that technology should serve the public good. Whether you're running models or running programs, your work intersects with the broader human condition. This book provides a way to navigate that intersection with skill, clarity, and responsibility.

Throughout the chapters, we'll explore real-world applications from public health and education to environmental justice and humanitarian response. We'll discuss the ethics of data use, the dangers of bias, and the importance of building trust. Most importantly, we'll focus on practice: how to design data projects that empower rather than exploit, illuminate rather than obscure.

The goal is not to simplify complex problems into metrics, but to bring a human-centered mindset to the digital tools we use to address them.

The journey starts here.

CHAPTER 1

Understanding the Mission of Data for Social Good

In recent decades, data has transitioned from a backend utility to a frontline force. It powers digital economies, drives decisions in healthcare and finance, and underpins innovation across almost every modern system. But when we turn this power toward social challenges poverty, inequality, displacement, education gaps, environmental degradation, the stakes are no longer measured in profits or efficiency. They are measured in lives.

To understand the mission of data science for social good, we must first reframe what "value" means. In the commercial world, value is often defined by user growth, speed, predictive accuracy, or revenue. But in the world of social good, value emerges from impact, trust, and transformation. It's not about how well an algorithm performs in a sandbox it's about how deeply it understands the community it's meant to serve.

This kind of work begins with perspective. It asks data scientists to step out of the comfort of controlled datasets and simulated environments, and into complex, often messy realities where data is incomplete, misrepresented, or entirely missing. It asks us to care about the quality of life of the people behind the numbers not just the quality of our models. It reminds us that people are not datapoints; they are layered, contextual, and evolving.

Working in this field requires proximity not just technical proximity to data sources, but human proximity to the stories, histories, and pain points embedded in those sources. It demands humility, because the community often resist quick classification or quantification. It demands collaboration, because sustainable change cannot be engineered in isolation. And it demands courage, because sometimes the insights we uncover challenge the very systems we work within.

The mission of data science for social good also involves reckoning with the legacy of exclusion and harm that data has often perpetuated. Biased datasets have reinforced racial profiling in policing. Predictive tools have denied people healthcare, insurance, and credit. Automated systems have prioritized the powerful and punished the poor all in the name of optimization. In response, this movement asserts that impact cannot be divorced from ethics. That fairness isn't a bonus feature, it's the foundation.

But this is not a book about what's broken. It is a book about what's possible when data science is led by compassion, shaped by accountability, and grounded in justice. It is a book about using data to ask better questions, to elevate silenced voices, to redistribute access, and to inform solutions that are co-owned by the communities they touch.

In this world, success is not measured by perfect models. It is measured by equitable outcomes. Whether a child stays in school. By whether a clinic receives vaccines before an outbreak. Whether a displaced family finds housing, safety, and a restored sense of agency. These are the metrics that matter.

Ultimately, the mission of data science for social good is not to rescue people with data. It is to work alongside them to listen, to learn, to support, and to shift power. To build a future where data serves not just the most connected, but the most vulnerable. To ensure that we are not only solving problems, but doing so in a way that protects dignity, strengthens community, and leaves no one out of the equation.

The Human Side of Data

Every number we collect, analyze, and visualize is a glimpse into someone's life. A temperature reading may represent a fever that a rural clinic cannot treat. A location pin might trace the final steps of a missing child. A score in an education database could determine whether a scholarship is awarded or denied. In a world driven by metrics, it's easy to forget that behind every dataset is a human story often fragile, complex, and invisible to the algorithm.

This is the great paradox of data science: it seeks to understand the world by simplifying it. But social reality doesn't fit neatly into columns. People are not clean inputs. Their lives are messy, interrupted by inequality, shaped by culture, and constrained by systems they didn't create. The role of data scientists working for the social good, then, is not to strip away that complexity, but to honor it. It is to treat datasets not as abstract inputs, but as echoes of real people whose lives matter especially when those people are poor, underserved, or historically excluded.

Too often, marginalized communities appear in datasets only when they are in crisis during conflict, after displacement, through disease, or poverty. This reactive approach to data erases their everyday realities, their resilience, and their dreams. It reinforces a narrative that they only exist in suffering, rather than as full citizens with voice and agency. A true social good approach to data insists on changing this lens. It demands that we see communities not just as beneficiaries, but as co-creators of the knowledge that defines them.

The human side of data also requires presence. It means showing up not just in spreadsheets, but in community meetings, in fieldwork, in listening sessions. It means asking not only what data do we need? but who needs to be heard? It means choosing not to move fast and break things, but to move thoughtfully and build trust.

Technology can accelerate harm when it forgets people. An algorithm built in isolation can exclude voices it was never trained to recognize. A data model that optimizes for efficiency can fail the elderly, the disabled, or the undocumented. In these moments, it's not the machine that fails, it's the mission. And to correct that failure, we must bring humanity back to the center of our process.

Empathy is not a technical metric, but it should be a design principle. We can code for efficiency, but we must also design for dignity. We must ask not only what works, but who is it working and who is it leaving behind? Only then can data serve as a tool for inclusion rather than exclusion, for healing rather than harm.

Data science for social good at its best is not about saving people. It's about standing with them using evidence not to overpower their voices, but to amplify them. It is about recognizing that people are the reason we do this work. And it is their lives, not our models, that must be the final measure of success.

Redefining Impact in a Digital World

In a world where dashboards glow with real-time insights and performance metrics are celebrated like milestones, it's easy to confuse activity with impact. Clicks, conversions, and correlations dominate decision-making, while the slower, deeper effects improved well-being, restored trust, systemic equity remain harder to capture. In the realm of social good, however, the traditional metrics of success often fail to tell the full story.

When data is used to serve commercial ends, the questions are clear: What's the return on investment? How can we scale faster? Which product outperforms its competitor? But when data is deployed to address social challenges, those questions must shift. What does it mean to build safer communities? How do we measure dignity, inclusion, or empowerment? Can we prove that a predictive model prevented a child from dropping out of school or a life from being lost?

The answer is rarely found in a single data set. Social impact is layered and nonlinear. A well-designed intervention may take months or years to show results. A program may spark meaningful change in ways no metric can fully quantify. It may restore agency, deepen relationships, or shift public narratives. These are not statistical outliers, they are the very outcomes that matter most.

Redefining impact requires us to resist the temptation of speed and neat conclusions. It demands patience. It challenges the idea that bigger data is always better, or that models must be perfect before they're meaningful. In this world, a small dataset rooted in lived experience may carry more truth than a massive one built from abstracted assumptions.

This redefinition also requires a broader lens on value. An early warning tool for landslides isn't successful because it's 95% accurate, it's successful if it reaches the right people, at the right time, with the right action. A disease surveillance model is not impactful because it predicted an outbreak it is impactful if it triggered a coordinated response that saved lives. In the digital world, outcomes are often shaped by systems far beyond the algorithm. That's why partnerships, policy, and trust are as critical as precision.

Accountability matters, too. Data for social good should never be reduced to a one-way extraction where communities are surveyed, measured, and analyzed but never engaged. Real impact includes feedback. It includes participation. It includes ensuring that communities understand how their data is being used and can shape the outcomes that affect them. Anything less risks replicating the very injustices we claim to solve.

To redefine impact is not to lower standards. It is to raise deeper, more honest ones. It is to embrace a multi-dimensional understanding of what success looks like not only through numbers, but through narratives, relationships, and long-term transformation. It is to ask ourselves, consistently: Whose lives are we improving? How do we know? And how will they define success not just us?

From Charity to Measurable Change

For years, much of the work around doing good whether through aid, philanthropy, or development has been framed as an act of charity. A well-intentioned effort to give, to fix, or to help, often delivered from positions of privilege to those perceived as powerless. Data, in this framework, becomes a supporting tool: used to justify funding, count beneficiaries, or demonstrate benevolence. But this narrative, though familiar, is outdated and in many ways, dangerous.

Charity assumes a hierarchy: the giver and the receiver. It focuses on short-term relief rather than long-term transformation. It celebrates output meals delivered, well-built, tablets distributed while often ignoring whether those interventions addressed root causes or reinforced systemic inequities. When data is used to reinforce this model, it risks becoming extractive. Communities are surveyed, their pain quantified, their stories reduced to bullet points in a report. And then the data leaves with the researcher, the analyst, and the donor.

The shift from charity to measurable change requires a fundamentally different posture. It centers justice, not generosity. It insists that the people most affected by a problem must help define the solution. It treats communities not as passive recipients of aid, but as active co-creators of data, insight, and strategy. In this framework, the role of the data scientist is not to swoop in with answers, but to stand beside communities, to build tools with them not just for them.

This shift also requires clarity on what we mean by "measurable change." Not change that simply satisfies donors or stakeholders, but change that is real, felt, and sustained by the people on the ground. It might mean fewer maternal deaths, higher school retention, more equitable access to government services. But it could also mean fewer tangible things, greater trust in public institutions, a stronger sense of voice, or a community's ability to organize using their own data. These aren't side effects. They are the essence of impact.

To make this shift work, we need systems of accountability that flow in all directions not just from implementers to funders, but from communities to institutions, and from data users back to data sources. We need tools that don't just analyze problems but empower local actors to advocate, design, and act. We need data that doesn't just describe the world as it is but inspires the world as it could be.

From charity to measurable change is not just a slogan. It is a call to reimagine what data science looks like when equity is the goal not efficiency. It is an invitation to reject the idea that scale always equals success. And it is a challenge for everyone working in this space: to measure not just what's easy, but what's meaningful. To show not just that something happened, but that something truly changed and that the people most affected by it had a voice in making it so.

CHAPTER 2

Foundations of Data Science in the Public Sphere

Before data science can be meaningfully applied to public challenges, we must understand its foundations technically, ethically, and structurally. Unlike corporate settings where efficiency and profit dictate the rules of engagement, public-sector data science lives in a different context. It contends with public trust, bureaucratic complexity, under-resourced systems, and the lived experiences of millions of people who may never have opted into being analyzed in the first place.

At its core, data science is the discipline of extracting insights from data through a blend of statistics, computing, and domain knowledge. In practice, it involves collecting data, cleaning it, modeling patterns, and drawing conclusions that support decision-making. But when data is collected from public systems, schools, hospitals, courts, housing registries the consequences of error are not financial; they are human. A false prediction in a marketing model might cost a company money. A false prediction in a welfare model might cost a person their safety net, housing, or access to food.

This is why the public application of data science demands a different kind of rigor not just technical precision, but ethical integrity. It is not enough for a model to work. It must be fair. It must be explainable. It must serve people who have historically had little say in how decisions are made about them. These are not secondary concerns. They are foundational.

One of the most important tools in public-sector data work is transparency. Unlike private companies, which may treat their algorithms as proprietary, public institutions are accountable to the people they serve. When an algorithm influences school admissions or healthcare prioritization, communities have a right to understand how those decisions were made. This openness is not just a matter of principle it's a prerequisite for legitimacy.

Another key element is partnership. In the public sphere, no data scientist works alone. Effective data projects involve social workers, policymakers, activists, and citizens. They require an understanding of local norms, political climates, and institutional histories. A technical sound model that doesn't reflect local realities can do more harm than good. Collaboration ensures that data-driven solutions are grounded in context and guided by those who know the terrain best.

But for all its promise, the use of data in public institutions is often constrained. Many systems still rely on paper records. Infrastructure is weak, funding is scarce, and talent is often underdeveloped or overburdened. This makes it tempting to chase innovation for its own sake to deploy flashy tools that promise rapid transformation. But the real impact in the public sphere is rarely quick. It is slow, deliberate, and requires long-term investment in people, systems, and governance.

The foundational principle that must guide all data science in the public sphere is equity. Public systems must not only serve everyone they must especially serve those who have been left behind. This means being aware of how data is collected, who is missing from the records, and how historical biases may be embedded in the system. It means asking not just can we model this? but what does this model reinforce, and who might it disadvantage?

Data science for social good is not just about building better tools. It's about building better institutions, ones that see people not as problems to be solved, but as partners in the work of creating fairer, more inclusive societies. It's about using data not to predict what people will do, but to imagine what systems could do differently.

This foundation is both technical and moral. It is rooted in code, but also in conscience. It is shaped not only by what is measurable, but by what is meaningful. And it reminds us always that in the public sphere, the ultimate measure of success is not how much we know but how wisely we act on it.

Core Tools and Techniques

Data science is not magic. It is a craft built on methodical tools and techniques that help us transform raw information into actionable insight. When applied in the public sphere, the goal is not to impress with complexity, but to generate clarity, trust, and fairness. This means choosing tools that not only deliver technical accuracy but also adapt to the constraints and ethics of real-world use.

At the foundation lies data collection. Public sector data often originates from surveys, administrative records, satellite imagery, sensors, and open government datasets. But unlike private datasets, these are often incomplete, outdated, or inconsistently maintained. A census may have missing households. Health records may exist only in paper files. Data scientists working for social good must therefore be prepared to clean and structure datasets that were never designed for analytical use. This is not a one-time process, it's a practice of continuous interrogation and care.

Next is exploration data analysis (EDA). This is where the story beneath the surface begins to take shape. Using tools like Python (with libraries such as pandas, seaborn, and matplotlib), R, or even spreadsheet software for smaller contexts, analysts identify patterns, gaps, and anomalies. But in public-sector work, EDA goes beyond technical validation. It often requires asking: Does this pattern reflect truth or a systemic blind spot? Anomalies in data about underserved communities may reflect real disparities or may simply reflect that those communities were never fully counted in the first place.

When it comes to modeling, the techniques are familiar: regression, classification, clustering, time series forecasting. But the use case differs. Predictive models for social good must be interpretable, auditable, and accountable. A complex neural network might offer better accuracy, but if it cannot explain why, it flags a child as "at risk," it may not be appropriate for use in an education system. Techniques like decision trees, logistic regression, or explainable AI (XAI) methods are often favored not because they are simpler, but because they allow stakeholders to understand, question, and trust the outcome.

Equally critical is the process of validation. Public impact requires models that generalize well not just across datasets, but across populations and geographies. Cross-validation, fairness audits, and real-world trials become essential steps before any deployment. A model that works well in one district may fail catastrophically in another if cultural, linguistic, or socioeconomic differences aren't accounted for.

Lastly, visualization and communication play a defining role. Dashboards, reports, interactive maps, and infographics are the interfaces between data and decision-making. Tools like Tableau, Power BI, and open-source platforms like Superset or D3.js allow technical insights to be shared with nontechnical audiences. But the goal is never just to visualize data to tell the truth. In the public sphere, how your present data can influence public opinion, policy decisions, and even funding. That's a responsibility that must be carried with care.

Ultimately, the core tools and techniques of data science are not exclusive to the public sector. But their use in this space requires a mindset shift from optimization to inclusion, from speed to responsibility, from private gain to public value. Mastery of the tools is important. But mastery of intent is what sets this work apart.

Data Ethics and Responsibility

In the world of social impact, doing harm with data is often unintentional but that doesn't make it any less real. A model that denies someone access to a government benefit, an algorithm that flags a student as "high-risk," or a dashboard that visualizes personal health records without proper safeguards these are not just technical missteps. They are ethical failures. And they often affect the people with the least power to challenge them.

Data ethics begins with one simple but powerful truth: just because we can do something with data doesn't mean we should. The field of data science is filled with opportunities to scrape, predict, and analyze, but public trust is fragile. Once lost, it is difficult to rebuild. That's why responsibility is not a feature that can be added to a system later. It must be embedded from the beginning, starting at the moment data is collected.

Consent is the first ethical checkpoint. In many data-for-social-good projects, especially in humanitarian or crisis contexts, data is collected rapidly, with little time for informed engagement. Communities are asked to give information without a clear understanding of how it will be used, who will see it, or whether it will ever benefit them. True ethical practice means ensuring that consent is not just a checkbox, but a process of mutual understanding, revisited over time.

Beyond consent is the question of representation. Who is visible in the data? Who is consistently left out? Incomplete datasets can make marginalized populations disappear from the narrative. Worse still, biased data can reinforce harmful stereotypes. When a justice algorithm is trained on historic arrest data, it may be learned to criminalize poor neighborhoods, not because they are more criminal but because they have been policed more heavily. Without critical reflection, even the most accurate models can replicate injustice with terrifying precision.

Transparency is essential. In commercial contexts, algorithms may be hidden behind intellectual property. But in the public domain, the people have a right to understand how decisions are made especially when those decisions affect their lives. If a model determines which school a child attends or how aid is distributed after a flood, that model must be explainable. Data science in this context isn't just about outcomes, it's about trustworthiness.

Responsibility also means understanding power. Who gets to define the problem? Who controls the data? Who decides which indicators matter most? Ethics in data science isn't just about protecting individuals from harm, questioning the systems that produce harm in the first place. It's about confronting the fact that data collection has often been a tool of surveillance, not empowerment. And it's about building alternatives that center dignity and agency.

Finally, there's accountability. When a data system fails when it discriminates, leaks, or misleads who takes responsibility? Too often, harm is written off as "a bug" or an unintended side effect. But in data for social good, mistakes can't be quietly patched. They must be owned, investigated, and addressed in partnership with the affected communities. Being accountable means putting people before platforms. It means understanding that every model is a choice and every choice carries consequences.

In the end, data science is not neutral. The way we frame problems, select features, train models, and interpret results is shaped by our values, assumptions, and goals. If those values are not explicit and examined, they will default to the norms of the powerful. Ethics is the work of constantly surfacing those assumptions, challenging them, and choosing differently.

That is what responsibility looks like in the age of data: not technical perfection, but moral clarity. Not the absence of error, but the presence of care.

Building Public Trust through Transparency

Trust is the currency of every public system. It is what allows citizens to share personal information with governments, register for services, respond to surveys, and believe that the data they provide will be used in their best interest. In data science for social good, transparency is not just a technical requirement, it is a moral and civic imperative. Without it, even the most well-intentioned systems risk being viewed with suspicion, rejected by the public, or worse, weaponized against the very people they're meant to help.

Transparency begins with communication. People deserve to know how their data is being collected, what it will be used for, who will have access to it, and what safeguards are in place. In too many public-sector projects, data practices are hidden behind jargon, inaccessible policies, or opaque institutional language. Ethical transparency requires clarity. It means explaining complex systems in simple, honest terms whether to a village council, a parent group, or a community of displaced persons.

But transparency doesn't stop at collection. It extends through the entire lifecycle of a data project from cleaning and modeling to analysis and decision-making. If a model flags households for food aid, communities should know how the criteria were set. If a predictive tool is being used to determine school dropouts, educators and students should understand what indicators were used and how the tool will be monitored. Transparency invites public scrutiny not as a threat, but as a strength.

One powerful way to institutionalize transparency is through open data. When datasets, codebases, and evaluation methods are made public, they allow external actors researchers, watchdog groups, journalists, and citizens to validate claims, spot flaws, and improve systems collaboratively. Open data signals a willingness to be held accountable. It says: "We trust the public enough to let them see behind the curtain."

Transparency also involves acknowledging limitations. No model is perfect. No dataset is complete. When organizations admit uncertainty, they don't weaken their credibility, they strengthen it. They show that they are willing to engage with complexity, to listen to feedback, and to course-correct when necessary. This humility is essential to long-term public trust.

In high-stakes environments, where mistrust of authority is already high, transparency is especially critical. For example, in post-conflict regions or communities with histories of state abuse, a new data system even one designed to help may be met with fear. Here, building trust means going beyond information-sharing. It means involving communities in the design process, giving them control over how data is used, and ensuring they see the tangible benefits of participation.

Ultimately, transparency is not a single act. It is a practice a way of designing systems, communicating intentions, and staying accountable. It recognizes that data science does not happen in a vacuum. It happens in neighborhoods, in institutions, in histories shaped by power. And in those spaces, trust must be earned over time.

To build trust through transparency is to reject secrecy as standard. It is to believe that communities are not too uninformed to understand data, but too often excluded from it. It is to treat information not as a privilege, but as a public good. And in doing so, it lays the foundation for a more just, participatory, and equitable use of data where the people behind the numbers are never left in the dark.

CHAPTER 3

Identifying Problems Worth Solving

Not every data science project that can be done should be done. In a world flooded with information and endless technical possibilities, the most critical decision is often not how to solve a problem but which problem to solve. In the social sector, this choice carries even more weight. Poorly chosen problems can waste scarce resources, reinforce harmful narratives, or worse, direct solutions toward symptoms rather than root causes.

Identifying the right problems begins with listening. Too often, data practitioners enter communities with preconceived notions about what's broken and how to fix it. But lived experience rarely fits neatly into frameworks. What a dashboard flags as inefficiency might be a survival strategy. What an algorithm predicts as failure might be the product of systemic exclusion. Without meaningful community input, even well-designed interventions can solve the wrong thing or create new problems entirely.

Listening means engaging stakeholders from the start: local leaders, educators, health workers, and the very individuals the system aims to serve. It means surfacing the quiet problems that aren't always visible in the data but are deeply felt. It means being open to uncomfortable truths, like the fact that some systems weren't designed to be improved; they were designed to exclude.

Good problem definition also requires a shift in mindset. In commercial spaces, problems are often framed around optimization how to increase clicks, reduce churn, boost efficiency. In contrast, social problems are messy, political, and entangled. They involve histories of injustice, overlapping crises, and complex human behavior. A school dropout is rarely the result of a single factor. A spike in hospital visits might signal a lack of clean water, not a failure of medical systems. The role of the data scientist here is to zoom out before zooming in to understand the ecosystem, not just the event.

Context matters. A "problem" in one setting may be a solution in another. For example, informal markets may appear disorganized in datasets, but they are often sophisticated systems of mutual support. Street hawking may be labeled as illegal commerce, but for many families, it is a lifeline. Treating such dynamics as problems to be "corrected" without understanding their role in community survival is a form of digital colonization where models override context instead of learning from it.

Ethical problem selection also involves questioning who benefits from the solution. A predictive policing model may reduce crime statistics, but if it intensifies surveillance in poor neighborhoods, it does more harm than good. A model that predicts which students will fail may help schools allocate resources but if it leads to tracking or exclusion, it risks stigmatizing the very children it aims to help. In each case, identifying a problem must include identifying its potential for unintended consequences.

This is where equity becomes central. A problem worth solving in data for social good is one that addresses disparity, promotes dignity, and shifts power. It is not merely about what's efficient, but about what's just. It is not about charity or saviorism, but about solidarity and co-creation. The best problems to work on are often defined not by data availability or algorithmic challenge, but by community demand, urgency, and the potential for long-term transformation.

At its heart, problem identification in this field is a moral act. It is an invitation to slow down, to go deeper, and to let humility guide innovation. It is a commitment to value listening over labeling, partnership over prediction, and people over patterns. And when done right, it becomes the cornerstone of data science that not only works but truly matters.

Community-Centered Problem Discovery

Every meaningful data project begins not with a spreadsheet, but with a conversation. Long before the first variable is defined or the first model trained, there is a moment often informal where a problem begins to take shape. In the world of social good, this moment must begin with the community.

Community-centered problem discovery is both a methodology and a mindset. It shifts the focus from external diagnosis to internal definition. Instead of asking, "What's wrong here?" the process begins with "What matters most to the people living this experience?" The role of the data scientist becomes that of a listener, a translator, and a collaborator rather than a fixer or evaluator.

This approach challenges traditional power dynamics. In many projects, data experts and decision-makers operate far from the people their models affect. They rely on secondhand information, government reports, or indicators pulled from large datasets. But these sources, while helpful, are rarely complete. They often miss nuance, misclassify behaviors, and ignore histories of exclusion. Community-centered problem discovery fills that gap. It treats the people closest to the issue as experts in their own right.

Listening well means creating space for qualitative data: interviews, focus groups, community forums, lived testimony. It means understanding that what a community values may not always align with what institutions measure. For example, a maternal health project might aim to reduce mortality rates, but a community may be more concerned with access to respectful care, language interpretation, or the presence of midwives they trust. A school system might define success through standardized test scores while parents may prioritize safe environments and mental well-being.

These insights are not peripheral, they are foundational. They reveal the social, cultural, and emotional context that raw data often hides. They help frame problems in terms of lived reality, not just policy goals. And they ensure that any data science solution is grounded in relevance, not assumption.

Moreover, involving communities early helps prevent extractive practices. Too often, communities are only consulted after data has been collected and decisions have been made. They are asked to validate conclusions they had no part in shaping. Community-centered discovery reverses that timeline. It builds relationships, creates transparency, and lays the groundwork for informed consent and long-term trust.

This process also requires humility. Sometimes what a data scientist sees as a problem may not be seen that way by the community at all. A high level of informal labor might signal economic vulnerability in a dataset but on the ground, it may represent resilience and autonomy. The work is not to impose definitions, but to listen and learn. This does not mean avoiding analysis. It means anchoring analysis in context.

When communities are invited to help define problems, they are more likely to stay engaged in the process of solving them. Ownership increases. Accountability deepens. And the resulting data work whether it involves predictive analytics, data visualization, or impact evaluation becomes not just technically valid, but socially meaningful.

Community-centered discovery is not a detour. It is the foundation. It is the discipline of asking better questions so that the answers we generate serve real lives not abstract assumptions. It is how we ensure that data science, no matter how advanced, never loses its grounding in human reality.

The Role of Qualitative Research

In a discipline often driven by numbers, trends, and large-scale patterns, qualitative research may seem like an afterthought. But in the pursuit of social good, it is anything but optional. It is essential. Qualitative research gives us what raw data cannot: voice, context, contradiction, and emotion. It fills in the blanks that spreadsheets overlook and brings human complexity to the surface.

While quantitative analysis can tell us what is happening, qualitative research helps us understand why. It explains the decision behind a dropout, the feeling behind a migration, the fear behind an unreported illness. It reveals not just outcomes, but motives, barriers, and lived experiences factors that are often unmeasurable but critically important in designing effective, ethical interventions.

In the early stages of problem discovery, qualitative research is especially valuable. It helps unpack how a community defines a challenge in its own terms, what solutions it has already tried, and what trade-offs it faces daily. Focus groups, narrative interviews, ethnographic observations, and participatory design workshops all offer windows into realities that might otherwise remain invisible. These methods don't just extract insight, they build relationships. They affirm dignity. And they open channels for collaborative sense-making.

Qualitative insights also serve as a check on bias. Models and metrics are shaped by assumptions. Without the grounding of real voices, data scientists may misinterpret what they see. A dip in attendance rates might be explained by transportation issues, caregiving responsibilities, or cultural practices that a numeric pattern alone cannot clarify. Listening to stakeholders, the students, the parents, the teachers brings depth and direction to the analysis. It ensures that models are not only technically sound but socially coherent.

Moreover, qualitative research helps us uncover what's missing in the data. Many communities that face marginalization are underrepresented in official datasets or misrepresented altogether. In refugee settlements, informal housing, or nomadic regions, data may be sparse or outdated. In such contexts, stories are often the most reliable source of truth. They reveal the contours of a problem before a baseline can be quantified. They help frame the questions before answers are sought.

Importantly, qualitative research does not compete with quantitative methods, it complements them. It offers texture where numbers provide scale. Together, they form a fuller picture. In mixed-methods research, this balance allows practitioners to validate findings, adjust model assumptions, and ensure that interventions resonate on the ground. A survey might indicate that 70% of respondents lack access to health care; interviews might reveal that mistrust, language barriers, or gender norms are the underlying cause.

For data science to truly serve the public good, it must be grounded not only in statistical logic but in human meaning. It must recognize that knowledge is not only embedded in datasets, but in dialogue. And it must value the expertise of those who live the problem not just those who analyze it.

Qualitative research reminds us that social impact is not built on abstraction. It is built on understanding. And in that understanding lies the foundation for more relevant, respectful, and resilient data-driven solutions.

Prioritizing Equity in Data Selection

In data science, what we choose to collect or ignore signals what we value. Every dataset is a mirror of priorities. And too often, it reflects a world where the most vulnerable are least visible. In the work of social good, equity in data selection is not a technical step. It is a moral commitment. It determines whose realities are counted, whose stories are legitimized, and whose needs shape the outcome.

Equity starts with inclusion. Traditional data systems often leave out entire populations: undocumented individuals, informal workers, people with disabilities, nomadic communities, and those without digital footprints. These omissions are rarely accidental. They are a consequence of systems built without the participation or even the consideration of those who fall outside dominant norms. When left unaddressed, these gaps lead to solutions that work only for those already seen.

To prioritize equity, we must deliberately seek out the silenced. This requires designing collection strategies that reach beyond convenience sampling or centralized records. It may involve working with grassroots organizations, deploying mobile survey teams, translating tools into local dialects, or using audio instead of text for non-literate populations. It may also mean adjusting definitions so that what is counted truly reflects lived experience. For instance, income metrics may miss the value of informal economies; household surveys may ignore those without stable shelter.

Beyond whom is included, equity also shapes what is measured. Are we tracking what matters to institutions, or what matters to communities? Are we capturing only deficits, illness, crime, failure or also strengths, resilience, and local solutions? Too often, data about marginalized communities centers their struggles but not their contributions. An equitable approach asks: Are we reinforcing stereotypes, or challenging them? Are we defining people solely by their problems?

Prioritizing equity also means questioning how power shapes data collection. Who decides what gets measured? Who benefits from the findings? Who has control over the interpretation and application of the results? These questions push us beyond technical choices into structural ones. They remind us that equity is not just about fairness in sampling it's about fairness in influence, voice, and representation throughout the entire data lifecycle.

Moreover, equity in data selection demands care in how gaps are addressed. It is tempting to "fill in" missing data with algorithms or proxies. But if the gap represents a systemic exclusion, no amount of imputation can make it fair. Sometimes, the ethical response is not to model around the absence, but to acknowledge it and ask why the absence exists in the first place.

Transparency is vital in this process. Practitioners must be honest about who is present in the data and who is not. They must document limitations, surface blind spots, and invite scrutiny. This vulnerability is not a weakness. It is a sign of rigor and integrity and an acknowledgment that equity is not a checkbox, but an ongoing discipline.

In the end, equitable data selection is about designing systems that reflect everyone's humanity not just those at the center of power. It's about refusing to treat invisibility as neutrality. And it's about ensuring that the problems we identify and the solutions we build are grounded in justice, not just efficiency.

CHAPTER 4

Data Collection in Low-Resource Environments

Data is often described as the new oil an abundant and valuable resource. But in many parts of the world, especially in low-resource environments, data is more like clean water: scarce, hard to collect, and essential for survival. In humanitarian contexts, rural areas, informal settlements, and underfunded systems, the challenge isn't just how to analyze data it's how to collect it in the first place. And how to do so in ways that are ethical, inclusive, and effective.

Low-resource environments present unique obstacles to data collection. These include infrastructural limitations, like the absence of stable internet, electricity, or transportation; institutional limitations, such as weak civil registries or fragmented health systems; and social limitations, including language diversity, literacy barriers, mistrust of institutions, and cultural sensitivities. Together, these factors can result in incomplete, outdated, or biased datasets and they can severely limit the effectiveness of models trained elsewhere.

But these challenges do not make data work impossible. They make it different. They demand creativity, humility, and deep community engagement. They require an adaptive mindset one that sees limitations not as roadblocks, but as design constraints to be respected and worked with, not against.

One of the most powerful tools in these contexts is participatory data collection. Rather than parachuting in with top-down surveys or imported tools, participatory methods involve communities in shaping the data process. This includes defining questions, designing instruments, and sometimes even collecting and interpreting the results. When people are part of the process, the data becomes more accurate, more trusted, and more likely to be used for local advocacy.

Mobile technology has also transformed what's possible. In areas where traditional infrastructure is lacking, SMS surveys, USSD tools, and offline apps allow data collection to occur on a scale, even without internet access. Open-source tools like Kobo Toolbox and ODK (Open Data Kit) are widely used in humanitarian and development settings. They enable enumerators to collect data offline and upload it later, ensuring continuity even in volatile environments.

Still, technology is not a substitute for trust. In many low-resource settings, there is deep skepticism about data collection often based on historical abuses or unfulfilled promises. Extractor research has created fatigue and suspicion. In such contexts', building trust is as important as building a sample frame. This means working with local leaders, hiring community members as enumerators, and communicating openly about why data is being collected, how it will be used, and what the community can expect in return.

Data security and privacy also take on heightened importance in these settings. When individuals have limited legal protection or digital literacy, the risk of harm from data misuse increases. Special care must be taken to ensure informed consent, anonymize sensitive information, and avoid collecting unnecessary data that could put people at risk. Just because data is hard to come by doesn't justify collecting more than is ethically needed.

Importantly, data collection in low-resource environments is not just about the present it is about building systems for the future. Whenever possible, efforts should leave behind tools, training, or processes that enable ongoing, community-led data practices. Capacity-building is not an add-on. It is a core feature of any sustainable, socially responsible data initiative.

In the end, working in low-resource environments tests more than your technical skill. It tests your commitment to inclusion, to listening, and to equity. It reminds us that those with the least access to data are often those who need it most not just to be counted, but to be seen, heard, and empowered to shape their own futures.

Working Without Perfect Infrastructure

In much of the world, data infrastructure is neither digital-first nor centrally managed. Paper records still dominate health systems. Electricity is intermittent. Internet access is limited to urban areas, and even then, often unstable. Devices are shared. Storage is manual. And yet data still gets generated. Decisions are still being made. Communities still organize, respond, and adapt. The question is not whether infrastructure is lacking. The question is how we design systems that work within and not despite these constraints.

The assumption that effective data science requires ideal infrastructure is a form of bias. It privileges environments that mirror corporate or academic labs and renders invisible the ingenuity of communities operating under conditions of scarcity. Working without perfect infrastructure means rejecting a one-size-fits-all model of data practice. It means designing for resilience rather than perfection.

One strategy is to decouple data collection from real-time connectivity. Offline tools, such as mobile-based survey apps, allow enumerators to gather information in remote locations and sync it later when the internet becomes available. This reduces dependency on constant power or network access, which may be impossible in conflict zones, rural villages, or after natural disasters. But building offline systems also means ensuring that data is properly secured until upload especially when sensitive information is involved.

Another key strategy is leveraging what already exists. In many communities, information is kept in hand-written ledgers, oral records, or community rosters maintained by local leaders. While these formats may lack standardization, they often contain vital, context-rich data. Converting such sources into usable datasets requires care: not just digitization, but interpretation. It means understanding how the data was recorded, what social norms influenced it, and where biases may have crept in. It also means recognizing that digitizing information does not automatically improve its quality or value.

Flexibility in tool design is also critical. Data collection platforms must work on low-end phones, with minimal data usage and offline capability. Interfaces should support local languages and consider literacy levels. Enumerator workflows should adapt to power outages, weather disruptions, or local events. A robust system is not one that avoids disruption, it's one that survives it.

Human infrastructure must not be overlooked. Where digital systems are fragile, relationships are strong. Community health workers, teachers, cooperative leaders, and traditional authorities often serve as informal data custodians. Collaborating with them not only increases accuracy it builds trust. In contexts where institutional trust is low, these actors may be the only bridge between data systems and community participation.

Infrastructural challenges also raise ethical questions. Should a fragile community network be burdened with high-frequency surveys just to meet donor expectations? Should people be asked to share data when they may not have access to its benefits or even a way to understand how it will be used? Responsibility in low-infrastructure environments requires more than technical ingenuity. It requires moral clarity.

Ultimately, working without perfect infrastructure is not a barrier, it's a design challenge. And it's an invitation to reimagine what's possible when data systems are built for equity, adaptability, and sustainability, not just scale. In these settings, simplicity is strength. Relationships are infrastructure. And innovation doesn't mean bringing in more often means doing more with less but doing it with care.

Mobile Surveys and Citizen Science

In contexts where traditional infrastructure is weak or entirely absent, mobile technology has emerged as a bridge not just between people and data systems, but between communities and visibility. With the rise of mobile phones, even in low-income and remote areas, new opportunities have emerged for gathering information quickly, affordably, and on a scale. At the heart of this shift are two powerful approaches: mobile surveys and citizen science.

Mobile surveys offer a flexible, low-cost way to collect data directly from individuals, often in their own languages and on their own devices. Using channels like SMS, USSD, voice calls, or mobile apps, organizations can reach thousands of people across distances that would otherwise be prohibitive. In health crises, conflict zones, and disaster responses, mobile surveys have enabled rapid needs assessments, service tracking, and feedback collection in real time.

But these tools are only as good as their design. In low-resource settings, mobile surveys must account for varying levels of digital literacy, intermittent network access, and cultural communication norms. For example, while a text-based survey might seem efficient, it may exclude respondents who are illiterate or unfamiliar with texting. Voice surveys or IVR (interactive voice response) systems though more expensive can increase accessibility. Similarly, questions must be simple, respectful, and relevant, avoiding technical jargon or assumptions about context.

Timing also matters. A survey sent during work hours may be missed. A follow-up message may feel intrusive if trust has not been established. In places where communities have been surveyed repeatedly without seeing any change, there can be deep skepticism. As a result, every mobile engagement must be designed with sensitivity prioritizing informed consent, clarity of purpose, and feedback mechanisms that let people know their input matters.

Citizen science takes a more participatory approach. Instead of asking communities to respond to predefined questions, it invites them to help define what's worth measuring and to actively participate in collecting and interpreting that data. This can involve tracking water quality in their villages, mapping unregistered homes using GPS, monitoring crop health, or documenting incidents of local conflict. With basic training and simple tools, ordinary people become data collectors and stewards of their own environments.

This approach empowers in ways that traditional surveys cannot. It builds ownership. It shifts the dynamic from extraction to collaboration. And it generates locally informed insights that external actors might otherwise miss. Citizen-generated data is particularly valuable in areas where government records are absent, unreliable, or politically sensitive. It can illuminate hidden realities, catalyze action, and provide early warning signals that top-down systems often fail to detect.

However, citizen science is not without challenges. Data quality must be addressed through training, supervision, and validation. Ethical questions about consent, safety, and privacy are heightened when non-professionals are gathering sensitive information. And the process takes time it requires relationship-building, transparency, and investment in capacity-building that outlasts the project cycle.

Still, the impact is profound. Whether through a farmer texting rainfall pattern, a youth group mapping informal waste sites, or a community documenting maternal death, mobile and citizen-powered methods redefine what it means to collect data. They turn systems that were once extractive into engines of empowerment.

In environments where connectivity is partial and systems are fragile; these methods remind us that people are not just subjects of data they are sources of knowledge. And when given the right tools and respect, they become agents of change in the very systems that once overlooked them.

Data Partnerships with NGOs and Local Governments

In low-resource environments, no single entity can solve complex problems alone. Data science for social good, particularly in these settings, thrives not on individual brilliance but on collective effort. NGOs, local governments, community organizations, and data practitioners all bring different pieces of the puzzle and only by aligning these pieces can lasting, meaningful solutions emerge.

Non-governmental organizations (NGOs) are often the closest to the ground. They understand the daily realities of the communities they serve; they speak the local languages both literally and culturally and they are trusted in ways that external actors may not be. NGOs collect valuable data through their programming, monitoring, and evaluations. Yet this data often remains siloed, unstandardized, or underutilized beyond reporting to funders.

Local governments, on the other hand, possess the mandate and infrastructure to scale impact across entire jurisdictions. They maintain registries, administer public services, and influence policy. However, in many low-resource settings, their data systems are outdated, fragmented, or plagued by capacity gaps. They may lack the technical staff, secure platforms, or reliable methods to extract insights from the information they hold.

This is where partnership becomes powerful. By combining the deep contextual knowledge of NGOs with the institutional reach of local governments and integrating the technical expertise of data scientists' new opportunities emerge to collect, analyze, and apply data in ways that are ethical, actionable, and locally grounded.

Effective partnerships begin with alignment. Data-sharing agreements must be built on clear, shared goals: What decision needs to be informed? What service needs to be improved? Who will use the insight, and how will the community benefit? When these questions are answered collaboratively, data collection becomes purposeful, not extractive. It becomes part of a solution not just a report.

Building these collaborations also requires trust. NGOs may fear that sharing data will expose them to scrutiny or loss of control. Governments may worry about transparency or revealing institutional weaknesses. Data scientists may struggle with inconsistent formats or access delays. Trust is earned by respecting each partner's role, addressing concerns openly, and emphasizing co-ownership of both the data and the decisions that result from it.

Interoperability is another critical factor. Many organizations collect similar data on education, health, gender, or access but use different tools, structures, or indicators. Without harmonization, these efforts lead to duplication or fragmentation. Creating shared data dictionaries, standardized templates, or regional platforms can improve coherence. But these technical solutions must be accompanied by shared training, governance frameworks, and ongoing dialogue to ensure that data flows responsibly and meaningfully.

Capacity-building must also be part of the equation. Partnerships should leave behind more than insights; they should strengthen the data literacy and systems of those involved. Whether that means training government officials in basic analytics, helping NGOs improve digital security, or developing local research talent, the goal is to create a stronger, more autonomous data ecosystem over time.

When done right, these partnerships unlock possibilities that no actor could achieve alone. They help detect emerging needs faster, allocate resources more effectively, and advocate for policies rooted in evidence. They also create a feedback loop between people, systems, and decision-makers making the data more reflective, responsive, and relevant.

Above all, partnerships in low-resource environments are a reminder that data science is not just about code. It's about connection. It's about building the human infrastructure needed to make data useful, safe, and impactful not only for those who hold power, but for those who live with its consequences.

CHAPTER 5

Cleaning Structuring and Humanizing Data

Once data has been collected, whether through mobile surveys, government systems, or citizen-led efforts, the work is far from over. Raw data is rarely usable as-is. It arrives messy, inconsistent, and fragmented. Some fields are blank. Others are duplicated. Values are mis entered, outliers go unchecked, and entire categories may be missing altogether. Before any meaningful analysis can begin, the data must be cleaned, structured, and most importantly humanized.

Cleaning and structuring data are technical acts. Humanizing it is an ethical one.

In practice, data cleaning involves identifying and addressing errors or inconsistencies. This may include removing duplicates, handling missing values, correcting formats, and standardizing entries. In the social sector, however, these tasks are not merely about producing tidy spreadsheets, they are about preserving meaning. For instance, a missing birth date in a rural health record may not be an oversight. It may reflect undocumented births, traditional naming ceremonies, or other cultural practices that influence data reporting. To "fix" such a value without context is to overwrite a story with a shortcut.

Structuring data means organizing it in ways that support analysis. This may involve creating relational databases, generating unique identifiers, or transforming data from wide to long formats. In government systems, this process can be deeply challenging. Records may exist in multiple formats, across unconnected agencies, and with varying levels of quality. Yet thoughtful structuring creates the foundation for interoperability and reuse. It allows health, education, and social protection systems to "speak" to one another and in doing so, to serve people more holistically.

But cleaning and structuring alone are not enough. Without humanizing the process, data work risks becoming mechanical. It begins to treat people as datapoints things to be sorted, filtered, and modeled. That is when decisions become dangerous. When a student is flagged as "low performing" based on a score, or when an entire community is deemed "high-risk" by a flawed model, the consequences are not theoretical. They shape lives.

Humanizing data starts by asking: What does this data represent? Who provided it? Under what conditions? And what context is missing from these numbers? It means pausing to understand why an anomaly exists instead of deleting it. It means retaining "messy" data when that messiness reflects real-world complexity.

This approach is especially critical when working with marginalized populations. Data about refugees, informal workers, or undocumented individuals may be incomplete not because they are unreliable, but because they operate outside systems designed without them in mind.

Discarding such records because they do not meet a neat standard only reinforces their invisibility.

Humanizing data also involves how we talk about it. Terms like "data cleaning" can imply that the raw information is dirty or flawed when in reality, it is a reflection of people living within constraints. The act of transforming that data should not erase those realities but preserve them. Our responsibility is not just to make data useful, but to keep it honest.

Ethical cleaning and structuring practices include documenting every step taken, what was changed, why it was changed, and what assumptions were made. Transparency in preprocessing ensures that others can replicate the work and that communities can understand how their information has been used or transformed. In public data work, this level of openness builds trust.

Finally, humanizing data means recognizing that no dataset is ever complete. There are always missing voices, blind spots, and limitations. The goal is not perfection, but respect. The process of cleaning and structuring should be guided not just by efficiency, but by empathy. Not just by models, but by meaning.

Because when we remember that data is not just input it is insight from lived experience, we begin to handle it with the care it deserves. And we ensure that every line of code, every query, every model starts from the same place: with people.

From Raw to Usable: A Technical Perspective

At the heart of every impactful data project lies a fundamental truth: raw data is not ready data. Before any visualization, prediction, or decision-making can take place, raw inputs must be transformed into structured, reliable formats that can support analysis. This process often overlooked or undervalued is one of the most important and time-intensive parts of the data science workflow, especially in public interest contexts where data is rarely clean, complete, or consistent.

In technical terms, working with raw data means confronting messiness. Fields may contain free-text entries, inconsistent units, malformed dates, or typos. Duplicate records may exist under different names. Categorical values may vary in spelling or case. Numerical entries may fall outside plausible ranges. These issues are not nuisances, they are signals. They reveal the conditions under which data was collected, the systems it passed through, and the assumptions embedded in its design.

The first step in transforming raw data is data profiling: a comprehensive assessment of structure, completeness, and content. Profiling helps identify missing values, distribution skews, outliers, and data types. It surfaces questions like: What percentage of entries are missing? Are there values that defy logic? Is this column categorical or freeform? Profiling is not just about discovering errors, it's about understanding patterns and inconsistencies in context.

Once profiling is complete, cleaning begins. This includes handling missing data either by imputing values using statistical methods, flagging them explicitly, or leaving them blank if the absence holds significance. Categorical values are standardized, such as converting all instances of "Female," "F," and "fem" into a single, consistent format. Duplicates are identified and merged or removed based on logic. Outliers are assessed carefully flagged if suspicious, retained if meaningful.

At this stage, documentation is essential. Every cleaning decision whether a column was dropped, a value replaced, or a data type altered should be recorded. In social good contexts, transparency about these decisions is not just good practice; it is a matter of ethics. Communities, partners, and researchers need to understand how the data has been shaped before trusting the conclusions it supports.

Structuring follows cleaning. This includes organizing the dataset into consistent, analyzable formats. For tabular data, this might mean reshaping wide data (where each row holds many variables) into long data (where each row represents a single observation). For multi-source projects, it involves creating keys to merge tables across systems such as linking household data with service delivery logs. In geospatial datasets, structuring includes ensuring coordinate formats are accurate and mapped to the correct projection systems.

Validation rounds out the process. Here, data is tested for integrity and logic. Do the values sum to expected totals? Are there temporal anomalies? Do derived variables (such as age from date of birth) match known truths? This step ensures that cleaning didn't introduce new errors and that the data can be trusted downstream.

Tools matter. Languages like Python and R, with libraries such as pandas, dplyr, or data. table, offer powerful options for cleaning and structuring. Specialized platforms like OpenRefine can support visual data wrangling. For collaborative environments, Jupyter notebooks or RMarkdown files allow teams to combine code, commentary, and output in a reproducible workflow.

But no tool can substitute for judgment. Technical rigor must be paired with contextual awareness. Is this missing value a technical error or a systemic pattern? Does this outlier indicate data entry failure or a person with a real, exceptional experience? The best practitioners don't just clean for the sake of analysis. They clean with curiosity, care, and caution.

Transforming raw data into usable insight is not glamorous work. But it is foundational. And in the context of data for social good, it is also an act of responsibility. Because every cleaned column, every structured file, is one step closer to clarity. One step closer to justice. One step closer to impact that truly reflects the world as it is and helps shape it into what it could become.

Bias, Gaps, and Representational Fairness

All data is partial. It captures a slice of reality, shaped by who collected it, how it was recorded, and what was considered worth measuring in the first place. In public interest work, acknowledging this partiality is not just a technical concern, it's a moral responsibility. Because bias in data does more than skew results. It determines whose lives are legible, whose needs are visible, and whose stories are systematically ignored.

Bias often enters the dataset long before analysis begins. It starts at the moment of data collection: who was surveyed, who was left out, what categories were used, and how questions were framed. Structural inequalities like limited access to healthcare, the internet, or education can lead to entire populations being underrepresented in data systems. When these gaps are treated as neutral or accidental, we risk reinforcing the very inequities we claim to address.

Consider a public health dataset that captures patient visits from urban hospitals but omits rural clinics. A predictive model built on that data may prioritize urban health outcomes and completely miss trends in rural morbidity. Or take a dataset that records gender as binary male or female leaving no room for non-binary individuals to be counted. These are not oversights. They design decisions with real-world consequences.

Bias can also arise from imputation the process of filling in missing data. When values are inferred based on the average or dominant pattern, they may smooth over meaningful differences or erase marginalized experiences entirely. Likewise, when datasets are rebalanced or resampled to address class imbalance (as in machine learning), care must be taken not to eliminate the very anomalies that reflect injustice or need.

Addressing these gaps starts with asking: Who is not in the data, and why? This simple question opens the door to deeper inquiry. Are women underrepresented in employment records because of informal work patterns? Are indigenous communities missing from national statistics due to language barriers or mistrust of authorities? Are migrants overlooked because data systems are not designed to track mobility? These are not just technical problems. They are signals of exclusion.

Representational fairness means working to correct these exclusions not by artificially inflating numbers, but by designing more inclusive systems. It means expanding data categories to reflect lived identities. It means triangulating quantitative findings with qualitative narratives. It means prioritizing data collection in underrepresented regions or populations, even when doing so is logistically harder or less statistically convenient.

It also means resisting the urge to treat all data as objective. Algorithms trained on biased data will replicate that bias even if the code itself is flawless. A predictive model used in the criminal justice system, for example, may suggest higher risk scores for communities that have historically faced over-policing, not because of actual behavior, but because of the system's legacy. In such cases, the issue is not only data quality its structural injustice embedded in historical records.

Transparency is key. When presenting findings or deploying models, practitioners must clearly communicate where the data came from, what limitations it carries, and whose voices are missing. Assumptions should be surfaced, not buried. Models should be stress-tested for fairness, especially when they inform decisions that impact people's lives.

But representational fairness is not just about fixing what's broken, it's about reimagining how we collect and use data altogether. It's about shifting power. Moving from extractive practices to participatory design. Asking communities what they want to be counted for, and what success looks like on their terms.

Because fairness is not a filter applied at the end. It is a choice made at every stage from design to deployment. And in the work of social good, it is the difference between data that reinforces exclusion, and data that helps to repair it.

Making Data Accessible for Non-Experts

In the world of data science, technical fluency is often assumed. Analysts speak in columns and confidence intervals. Policymakers receive charts and dashboards. But the people most affected by data-driven decision-making community members, frontline workers, teachers, caregivers are often left out of the conversation, not because they are uninterested in data, but because the data was never designed with them in mind.

Accessibility is not a feature to be added after the fact. It is a responsibility. Making data accessible means presenting information in ways that non-experts can understand, question, and use. It means removing jargon without dumbing down the message. It means treating clarity not as simplification, but as a form of respect.

This starts with language. Datasets are full of cryptic labels, codes, and acronyms that make sense to statisticians but confuse others. A column labeled "HH_FM_INC_Q1" may mean something to the data engineer, but to a school principal or health worker, it's a barrier. Clear, intuitive naming alongside readable documentation transforms raw information into usable knowledge. Descriptions should explain what each variable means, how it was collected, and what limitations it carries.

Visualization plays a powerful role. Well-designed graphs, maps, and infographics can bring data to life, especially for those who don't read spreadsheets or statistical reports. But good design is not about aesthetics alone it's about function. Visualizations must be culturally appropriate, interpretable across literacy levels, and mindful of how people process information. A bar chart showing rising cases of malnutrition may be technically accurate, but if it doesn't suggest what action can be taken or whom to contact it's not empowering. Accessibility includes not just visibility, but usability.

Formats matter too. In many low-resource settings, internet access is limited. Hosting a sleek, interactive dashboard online may look impressive, but it may never reach the people who need it most. Sometimes, a laminated poster in a local clinic, a printed one-pager at a town hall, or a radio explanation in a local dialect can be more impactful than an elaborate platform. The format must match the context. The delivery must match the audience.

More than anything, accessibility is about dialogue. Communities should not just receive data they should be able to engage with it. Ask questions. Raise doubts. Share insight. This two-way relationship transforms data from a report into a resource. It opens the door for co-interpretation and participatory action planning. When communities see themselves reflected in the data, and understand how it connects to their lived experiences, they are more likely to trust it and act on it.

This is especially important in systems where people have historically been excluded or harmed by data. Accessibility is part of rebuilding that trust. It signals that data is not just for governments or donors. It's for everyone. And that everyone regardless of education level, profession, or connectivity deserves to be informed and equipped.

Making data accessible to non-experts is not a detour from real analysis. It is the final, critical step that turns analysis into impact. Because in the end, data that cannot be understood by those who need it most is not just inaccessible. It's incomplete.

CHAPTER 6
Designing Solutions that Serve the Marginalized

Designing solutions in data science is not simply about solving problems. It is about choosing whose problems to prioritize and whose experiences to center in the process. When the goal is social good, the responsibility becomes even greater. It requires us to recognize that those who have historically been excluded, misrepresented, or underserved are not just users or beneficiaries. They are partners. They are experts in the systems they navigate. They are the reason the work matters.

To serve marginalized communities, design must begin with respect. Respect for context. Respect for constraints. And most importantly, respect for lived experience. The people closest to the problem often understand it more deeply than the professionals trying to address it. Yet in many data-driven projects, they are consulted late or not at all. This leads to tools that are irrelevant at best and harmful at worst. A platform intended to improve school attendance may fail if it ignores why students miss class in the first place. A mobile app for farmers may be useless if it requires constant connectivity or literacy in a dominant language.

Empathy is not enough. It must be translated into design choices. This means asking hard questions at every stage. Are we designing for users with limited access to devices? Are we considering people who speak minority languages? Are we validating assumptions with real feedback from the field? It also means being cautious about default settings that reflect the biases of dominant groups. An algorithm that assumes urban behaviors as a baseline will miss the realities of rural life. A model trained on mainstream datasets may exclude people whose lives fall outside those norms.

Accessibility must be designed from the beginning. This includes not only physical and technical accessibility but also cognitive and cultural accessibility. Interfaces must be simple, but not simplistic. Visuals must communicate meaning without relying on color cues or dense terminology. Audio alternatives must be available where literacy is low. Time and again, inclusive design proves that when you design for those at the margins, you create better solutions for everyone.

Another key principle is transparency. Communities have a right to understand how data about them is being used. They should be able to question the outcomes, suggest improvements, and refuse participation without penalty. Too many solutions collect data without ever returning value to the people who contributed it. A solution that hides its logic, its risks, or its intent is not truly in the service of the public.

Collaboration is essential. Designing with communities rather than for them is not just a slogan. It is a process that demands patience, humility, and shared decision-making. Participatory design workshops, co-creation sessions, and iterative pilots can all create space for this collaboration. These are not add-ons. They are the foundation of ethical practice.

Designing for the marginalized also means anticipating harm. Every solution should go through a process of harm assessment. Could this tool be used to profile vulnerable people? Could it unintentionally stigmatize a group or reinforce existing inequalities? Are there protections in place if the tool fails or is misused? Serving the marginalized includes protecting them from risk.

Importantly, solutions must be sustainable and context aware. A shiny app that works for a few months is less valuable than a simple tool that communities can own, adapt, and use over time. This requires capacity-building, not just technology transfer. It involves training, handoffs, and long-term support that respects local autonomy. True service means designing for what will endure after the project ends.

Ultimately, designing solutions that serve the marginalized is not about lowering the bar. It is about raising the standard. It is about holding us accountable to the people who are least likely to be heard but most likely to be affected. It is about shifting the center of gravity away from convenience and toward justice.

When design is inclusive, transparent, and grounded in the realities of the people it aims to support, it does more than solve problems. It restores dignity. It builds trust. And it turns data science from a technical exercise into a powerful tool for shared progress.

Cultural Sensitivity in Modeling

Every dataset carries culture within it. Every model reflects the values, beliefs, and assumptions of the people who designed it. When working across communities and geographies, especially in data science for social good, it is not enough to strive for technical accuracy. Models must also be culturally sensitive. They must recognize that people do not live in universal norms. They live in contexts shaped by tradition, history, language, and power.

Cultural sensitivity in modeling begins with how data is framed. What one community sees as an acceptable behavior may be flagged as an anomaly in another. A household structure that appears unusual in one country may be standard in another. Attendance patterns, family roles, naming conventions, and even concepts like time and health vary across societies. When models are built without acknowledging these differences, they risk misclassifying normal behavior as problematic or overlooking important nuances entirely.

This sensitivity starts long before the model is trained. It begins with conversations. With asking questions that reveal what is considered respectful, what is considered offensive, and what is considered meaningful in that community. It involves reviewing variables through the lens of local knowledge. If a model uses mobile phone usage as a proxy for income, it must first confirm that phones are distributed in a way that aligns with that assumption. If it uses commute distance as a risk factor for school dropout, it must understand how children in that region travel, who they travel with, and what barriers they face that may not be reflected in distance alone.

Even the mathematical structures of models can carry bias. A clustering algorithm may divide groups based on patterns that hold in data from a dominant population but break down when applied to a smaller or structurally different group. A language model trained in dominant dialects may fail to interpret text written in regional phrasing or nonstandard syntax. These are not technical failures. They are cultural blind spots.

Building culturally sensitive models requires diverse teams. The people designing the system should include those who understand the lived experience of the users. This may mean involving local analysts, community partners, or even training local youth to participate in the modeling process. It also means reviewing models not only with data scientists, but with teachers, health workers, social workers, or elders who can spot issues that no spreadsheet will reveal.

Sensitivity also means being transparent about limitations. A model may work well in one cultural context but require retraining in another. Developers should be honest about this. They should resist the temptation to generalize results without validation. They should document the cultural assumptions baked into each step and invite local feedback before deployment.

Validation itself must go beyond metrics like precision and recall. Community validation asking people whether the model reflects their reality is just as important. This can be done through pilot tests, participatory reviews, or even story-based evaluations that compare predictions to lived experience.

Cultural sensitivity also involves knowing when not to model. Some behaviors, identities, or situations are too complex, too private, or too sacred to be reduced to variables. In those cases, restraint is a form of respect. Knowing the limits of modeling is as valuable as knowing its potential.

Ultimately, cultural sensitivity is not about avoiding difference. It is about honoring it. It is about designing systems that work with the grain of local life, not against it. It is about recognizing that people's experiences are not noised to be cleaned from the data but meaning to be understood within it.

When we build models that reflect the worlds people actually live in, we build tools that earn trust, do less harm, and deliver deeper impact. That is the promise of cultural sensitivity in modeling not just better data science, but more just and human data practice.

Preventing Algorithmic Harm

Algorithms are powerful. They help sort information, detect patterns, and guide decisions at a speed and scale humans alone cannot manage. But that power, if misapplied, misinformed, or unchecked, can cause real harm. And when the people affected by that harm are already marginalized, the consequences are often invisible until it is too late. Preventing algorithmic harm is not just a technical challenge. It is a question of ethics, design, and accountability.

Harm can take many forms. It may be direct, such as when a credit scoring model denies a loan to someone because their zip code correlates with historic discrimination. It may be indirect, like when a predictive policing tool increases surveillance in low-income neighborhoods, leading to more arrests not because of rising crime, but because of heightened monitoring. It may be psychological, such as when students or patients are classified as failures by systems that do not account for their realities. It may be silent, as when certain groups are left out entirely and never appear in the data used to decide who deserves help.

The first step to preventing harm is recognizing that all models are built on assumptions. They reflect decisions about what to include, what to exclude, and what to optimize for. A model that values efficiency may prioritize speed over fairness. A model that minimizes error rates overall may ignore how those errors are distributed across race, gender, or geography. Harm often arises not from malice, but from misalignment between model logic and human values.

To prevent harm, models must be stress-tested for fairness. This means evaluating not only how accurate they are, but for whom they are accurate. It means disaggregating results across subgroups to reveal patterns of bias or exclusion. It involves looking for false positives and false negatives and asking who bears the cost of each mistake. A model that misclassifies a child as at risk might lead to unnecessary intervention. A model that misses a real need might leave someone without support.

Transparency is essential. Communities deserve to know when algorithms are being used to make decisions that affect them. They have a right to ask what data was used, how the model works, and how they can appeal if they disagree. Black-box models may be acceptable in other industries, but in the context of public services or humanitarian work, opacity is dangerous. People should not be governed by systems they cannot see or understand.

Involving communities in the design and testing of models can also reduce harm. When those with lived experience are invited to challenge assumptions, suggest variables, and validate outputs, models become more grounded. They reflect the real-world complexity that often escapes mathematical representation. Participatory modeling is not just good practice. It is good ethics.

Another important practice is designing redress. No model will be perfect. Mistakes will happen. Systems must include ways for people to contest decisions, correct errors, and recover from harm. This is especially important for populations with limited access to legal recourse or institutional support. When someone is misclassified, they should not be left to navigate a complex system alone. The burden of correction should never fall entirely on the person harmed.

Preventing harm also means resisting the pressure to deploy models before they are ready. Just because a tool is technically functional does not mean it is socially safe. Testing in the lab is not the same as testing in the field. Pilots should be monitored closely, and rollouts should be gradual, with built-in pauses for review and feedback. Ethical patience is better than rushed precision.

Ultimately, preventing algorithmic harm is about protecting people, not just refining code. It is about designing with care, deploying with humility, and responding with responsibility. In data science for social good, where trust is fragile and the stakes are high, that responsibility cannot be optional. It must be built into the system from the start.

Because algorithms can help us do incredible things. But only if we remember that behind every line of code is a life. And every life deserves safety, fairness, and the dignity of being treated as more than a datapoint.

Designing with the End-User in Mind

No matter how advanced a tool may be, no matter how elegant its code or impressive its model accuracy, a data solution is only as effective as its ability to be understood, trusted, and used by the people it is intended to help. Designing with the end-user in mind is not a stage at the end of development. It is a guiding principle that must shape every step from conception to deployment.

The term end-user is often treated as a technical placeholder, but in practice, it refers to people with names, routines, fears, and goals. It includes the health worker in a rural clinic who needs real-time alerts about supply shortages. It includes the teacher navigating attendance records in a low-connectivity environment. It includes the single mother checking her eligibility for a social benefit through her basic mobile phone. These individuals do not need cutting-edge interfaces. They need tools that make their lives easier, not more complicated.

Designing with the end-user in mind begins with listening. It requires understanding how people interact with information in their daily lives, what technologies they already use, what constraints they face, and what their expectations are. It requires field testing and feedback loops that allow for changes based on how real people respond, not how developers imagine they should respond.

Simplicity is key. This does not mean the tool must lack sophistication behind the scenes. Rather, it means that the front-facing experience should be intuitive, clear, and forgiving of mistakes. A user should not need a manual to understand a dashboard. A form should not reject someone because they entered a name differently than expected. Every interaction should respect the user's time, ability, and confidence.

Language is central to design. Interfaces should be available in the languages people speak and read. This includes not just translations, but localization ensuring that terms, instructions, and categories make sense in the cultural and social context of the user. Visual communication can also enhance accessibility, especially for users with limited literacy. Icons, color signals, and illustrations can carry meaning where text may not.

Designing for access also means anticipating obstacles. Can the tool function offline? Does it require high data usage? Is it readable on older phones or in areas with limited electricity? These questions should not be afterthoughts. They are design decisions. They are signals of whether a solution was truly created with the end-user in mind.

Trust must be earned. Users will not adopt a system they cannot understand or that has previously failed them. This is especially true in communities where data systems have been used for surveillance or exclusion. Building trust requires transparency. It means showing users how their data will be used, who will have access to it, and how they can take control. It also means delivering visible value. If people give their time, their data, or their feedback, they should see a result that benefits them directly.

Support is also part of the design. Help features, training guides, local contact points, and user communities can all reinforce successful adoption. No tool should assume that its design alone is enough. People need space to ask questions, to make mistakes, and to learn over time.

Finally, designing with the end-user in mind means being ready to let go of ideas that do not work. If a tool confuses more than it clarifies, it must change. If the original design assumed a need that does not exist, it must adapt. True human-centered design is not stubborn. It is responsive.

The most powerful data tools in the world will fail if they do not serve real people in real conditions. But when we design with care, listen with humility, and prioritize the lived experience of the end-user, we turn data into more than insight. We turn it into an agency. We turn systems into supports. And we turn design from a process of control into a practice of partnership.

CHAPTER 7
Case Studies from the Global South

Theory matters. Methods matter. But nothing illustrates the promise and challenges of data science for social good more clearly than real stories from the field. Across the Global South, communities, organizations, and governments are experimenting with ways to use data not just to inform decisions but to drive justice, inclusion, and local innovation. These efforts take place far from the well-resourced labs and think tanks that often dominate global narratives. Yet their impact speaks loudly, offering lessons on resilience, creativity, and co-creation.

These case studies are not perfect. They involve trade-offs, obstacles, and hard-earned progress. But they reflect what happens when data is used to meet people where they are and is shaped by those it is meant to serve. The Global South is not a passive recipient of data innovation. It is a proving ground for new approaches that prioritize equity over efficiency and human dignity over digital convenience.

In rural Uganda, a health initiative used simple mobile phones to track maternal health outcomes in areas where no formal electronic medical records existed. Expectant mothers were enrolled in a community-run program where they received automated voice messages in local languages with reminders about prenatal visits, nutrition tips, and emergency contact instructions. Community health workers recorded birth outcomes using feature phones, uploading data when they reached a connected area. Over time, this generated a live map of maternal health patterns, allowing the district health office to allocate midwives and supplies more strategically. This system did not require smartphones or high-speed networks. It relied on trust, local language support, and the recognition that data collection must work within people's realities, not outside them.

In the northeast of Brazil, a city facing high youth unemployment worked with civil society organizations and local universities to co-design a youth opportunity index. Rather than relying solely on census data or national employment figures, the team collected qualitative and quantitative data on barriers to employment. This included surveys on access to public transport, availability of mentorship, discrimination experiences, and digital literacy. Young people helped define the indicators and led the data collection effort. The resulting index became a planning tool for city officials, helping them design youth employment programs that reflect lived experience. Importantly, it also gave young people ownership of their narrative and a tool for advocacy.

In parts of India, farmers in low-income regions were facing unpredictable rainfall and declining crop yields. Satellite data on soil moisture and weather forecasts existed, but they were neither accessible nor understandable to smallholder farmers. A local nonprofit partnered with agricultural researchers and data scientists to create a simple alert system. Using text messages and voice prompts, the system translated technical insights into actionable advice when to plant, when to irrigate, when to expect storms. Farmers subscribed for free and received updates tailored to their crops and local conditions. The results were measurable: reduced crop loss, more efficient water use, and a sense of confidence built through information. This was not a big data platform in a conventional sense. It was small, precise, and rooted in language and trust.

In the Philippines, a coalition of activists and urban planners used participatory mapping to fight for land rights in informal settlements. Residents used GPS-enabled devices to map roads, schools, water points, and flood zones in neighborhoods that did not appear on official city maps. The data was then layered with government zoning plans to highlight inconsistencies and push back against eviction threats. What began as a grassroots effort became a formal data partnership, with the city agreeing to update its maps based on community-generated data. This case shows how data science can be a tool for citizenship, not just administration.

Across these stories, a common thread emerges. Impact does not come from flashy algorithms or cutting-edge platforms. It comes from humility in design, collaboration in process, and a willingness to adapt technology to context not the other way around. It comes from rejecting the myth that data must be big to be valuable. In many of these cases, small, focused datasets made a significant difference because they were trusted, timely, and tailored to local needs.

Case studies from the Global South remind us that data science is not a universal language. It speaks differently in different places. It must learn the accents of rural life, the codes of urban resilience, and the unwritten rules of cultural practice. And when it does, it stops being a distant science and starts becoming a local strategy for change.

These examples are not the exception. They are the future. A future where data serves not just efficiency, but equity. Not just systems, but people. And not just progress, but possibility.

Tackling Health Inequity in Sub-Saharan Africa

Health systems in Sub-Saharan Africa face a complex web of challenges: underfunded infrastructure, workforce shortages, geographic barriers, and historical inequities that limit access to care for millions. Yet amid these realities, there are powerful examples of how data is being used not just to monitor problems, but to drive more just and responsive health interventions.

One such effort took shape in northern Kenya, where maternal and child health outcomes remained deeply unequal across counties. In response, a regional coalition of public hospitals, health-focused nonprofits, and community health workers launched a decentralized data initiative. The goal was not simply to track births and deaths, but to understand why certain women were dying preventable deaths during childbirth while others were not.

Health workers were trained to collect real-time information using mobile devices at the point of care. This included antenatal visit frequency, complications during pregnancy, distance to the nearest facility, and patient-reported concerns. Rather than pushing this data upward to national dashboards alone, the program made it available at the facility and district levels. Nurses and midwives could see trends across time and location. They could respond before a case became critical.

The power of this approach lay in its ability to reveal invisible patterns. In one district, the data showed a sharp drop in postnatal care attendance during the rainy season. What appeared at first to be a health systems failure turned out to be a transport challenge. Roads were flooded, and women could not reach clinics on time. In response, local health administrators reallocated motorbikes and supplies to reach women at home. In another case, elevated rates of anemia were traced not to diet alone, but to the lack of iron supplements in rural pharmacies. Supply chains were restructured to address this.

Beyond logistics, the data exposed deeper structural inequities. In wealthier counties, women accessed ultrasound and emergency obstetric care as standard. In poorer ones, care was delayed or unavailable. These disparities were not new, but for the first time, they were mapped, shared, and acted upon in a coordinated way. District officials could no longer claim ignorance. The evidence demanded change.

Importantly, the project did not treat communities as passive subjects of analysis. Local leaders and traditional birth attendants were included in monthly review meetings. Their observations, drawn from daily interaction with families, were added to the data platform as qualitative notes. This integration of numerical and narrative data strengthened not just accuracy, but legitimacy. It also built a culture of accountability that extended beyond donor reporting to community trust.

The project faced limitations. Connectivity remained a barrier in some areas. Some frontline staff struggled with device maintenance or data fatigue. Privacy concerns emerged when sensitive data about sexual health was not adequately anonymized. But the team responded iteratively adjusting training, refining collection protocols, and simplifying dashboards based on user feedback. Over time, the system improved not because it was perfect, but because it was responsive.

The impact was tangible. Maternal deaths declined by double digits in some counties. Timely referrals increased. Community satisfaction with health services improved. But perhaps most significantly, the project redefined what equity in health data could look like not top-down audits from capital cities, but locally anchored insight that empowered nurses, families, and district planners alike.

Tackling health inequity in Sub-Saharan Africa requires more than funding and policy. It requires data systems that listen, adapt, and reflect the lived experience of those most at risk. When data is designed to be usable at the last mile, when it includes the voices of those it measures, and when it is used to close gaps rather than reinforce them, it becomes not just a record of inequality but a tool for justice.

Predicting Dropouts in Rural Education

In many parts of the Global South, school enrollment has improved dramatically over the last two decades. Yet staying in school remains a persistent challenge, especially in rural areas where poverty, family obligations, long commutes, and gender dynamics all contribute to high dropout rates. In these communities, the decision to leave school is rarely the result of a single moment. It is a slow erosion a gradual disengagement often missed until it is too late.

In eastern Zambia, a district-level education office partnered with a regional nonprofit and a local university to explore whether data could help identify students at risk of dropping out before it happened. The goal was not to punish or label students, but to intervene early with support tailored to the challenges they were facing.

The data came from school records that were already being collected: attendance, termly test scores, distance from home to school, age of entry, and basic household information. What made this project different was not the data itself, but how it was used. A team of local teachers and data analysts collaborated to build a simple predictive model that assigned a risk score to each student. The model was trained using three years of school data, looking at which combinations of factors most frequently preceded dropout.

The findings were revealing. Unsurprisingly, chronic absenteeism was the strongest predictor. But when layered with gender and household size, the patterns shifted. Girls from larger households who missed more than five days in a term were at significantly higher risk, often due to caregiving roles or household chores. Boys in certain villages dropped out not for academic reasons, but because of seasonal labor demands. These patterns were well known to the community, but the model helped quantify them and bring them into sharper focus.

Once risk scores were generated, they were shared privately with teachers and school administrators. No student saw their score. No labels were assigned. Instead, the data served as a guide for proactive check-ins, parent meetings, and small incentives like transport stipends or uniform support. In some schools, volunteers were recruited to walk long distances with students who had previously been walking alone. In others, peer mentorship programs were introduced.

The approach emphasized care, not surveillance. The model was not used to track or punish. It was used to prompt conversation. And critically, it was continuously updated with new data and teacher feedback, allowing it to improve over time.

There were challenges. Data quality varied from school to school. Internet access was weak, and many teachers were unfamiliar with spreadsheets or digital tools. The model had to be simplified and shared through paper reports during teacher training days. Some educators were skeptical at first, fearing judgment or additional workload. But once they saw the connection between the scores and their own observations, the tool became more than just numbers. It became a signal for support.

Over two academic years, dropout rates declined in the participating schools. But just as importantly, the culture around dropout prevention has shifted. Rather than reacting to absence after it became a pattern, teachers began asking questions earlier. Students reported feeling more seen and supported. Some schools even began collecting new data on transportation, mental health, and family stressors expanding the understanding of what affects learning.

This case highlights a core truth of data for social good. Prediction alone is not the point. What matters is how predictions are used and by whom. A model is only as ethical as the decisions it supports. In this case, the model served not as a gatekeeper, but as a bridge between data and human care.

Predicting dropouts in rural education does not require advanced technology. It requires listening, collaboration, and a deep respect for the lives behind the statistics. When those values guide the process, data can do more than describe a problem. It can help communities change their trajectory.

Informal Sector Mapping for Economic Inclusion

Across the Global South, the informal economy is not a fringe activity. It is the backbone of survival for millions. Street vendors, artisans, repair workers, transport operators, market traders, and unregistered service providers make up the majority of employment in many countries. These workers often operate outside formal regulation, without business licenses, tax records, or access to credit. As a result, they are frequently invisible to policymakers, excluded from financial systems, and vulnerable to displacement during urban redevelopment.

In Accra, Ghana, a city facing rapid urbanization and rising inequality, a coalition of urban planners, labor unions, and data scientists came together to address this invisibility. Their aim was to create a living map of the city's informal sector not just as a spatial exercise, but as a tool for recognition, inclusion, and advocacy.

The process began with street-level engagement. Rather than relying on satellite imagery or top-down surveys, the project hired youth from the neighborhoods in question to serve as mappers. These youth were trained to use mobile phones and open-source mapping tools to geotag informal businesses, record the type of service provided, estimate foot traffic, and gather basic information about needs and risks. The training process included workshops on data ethics, consent, and community dialogue, ensuring that the mappers were not just collectors, but trusted messengers.

Over three months, the project documented more than five thousand informal businesses in five districts of the city. The data revealed previously overlooked patterns. For example, informal vendors near bus terminals were providing more than half of the daily food access for commuters. Artisans clustered along certain streets had created networks of skill-sharing that were invisible in formal economic data. And several densely populated neighborhoods had thriving micro-enterprises that operated entirely in cash, with no access to formal banking.

Crucially, the data collection process was designed to benefit the workers as much as the planners. After each neighborhood was mapped, community meetings were held to validate the results and discuss priorities. Many workers expressed the desire not for regulation, but for recognition. They wanted safer public spaces, basic infrastructure like waste disposal, and protection from arbitrary eviction. The data gave them a platform to make these demands.

City officials were initially skeptical, concerned about legitimizing unregistered businesses. But when shown how informal vendors contributed to the city's daily economic functioning and how displacement would disrupt public food access and transport efficiency, they agreed to pilot more inclusive zoning policies. In one district, informal businesses were designated protected community trading zones. In another, micro-loans were extended through a partnership with a local bank using the mapping data to assess business density and viability.

The mapping effort also served as a financial bridge. Some vendors were introduced to mobile money platforms for the first time, supported by tailored onboarding workshops. Others used the data to negotiate for vendor associations to receive small infrastructure grants. What began as a spatial exercise evolved into an ecosystem shift bringing informal workers into conversations they had long been excluded from.

This case is a reminder that exclusion is not always the result of hostility. Sometimes, it is the result of the absence of being uncounted, unmapped, and unseen. But data can change that. When communities are equipped to tell their own stories in structured, credible formats, the data becomes not just an input for planning, but a lever for power.

Informal sector mapping is not about formalizing everyone. It is about understanding the economy as it truly exists and ensuring that the people who keep it alive are treated not as obstacles to be removed, but as citizens to be included. It is a practice rooted in dignity, visibility, and the belief that equity begins with acknowledgment.

CHAPTER 8

The Politics of Data Power Privacy and Policy

Data does not exist in a vacuum. It is collected, stored, analyzed, and acted upon within systems of power. Every data set reflects decisions about who is counted, what is measured, who controls the information, and who benefits from its use. In the work of social good, understanding the politics of data is not a distraction. It is a necessary part of ethical practice.

Power shows up at every stage of the data lifecycle. It shapes whose problems receive attention and whose realities remain undocumented. It determines which institutions get access to data infrastructure and which communities are expected to contribute without consent or compensation. It influences who builds the algorithms, who interprets the findings, and who gets to say whether the insights are valid.

This dynamic is especially sharp in contexts where data is used to make decisions about public services. For example, predictive models may determine where to allocate teachers, who qualifies for health benefits, or which communities receive early warning alerts. While these systems can improve efficiency, they also risk reinforcing existing inequalities especially when the people affected have no voice in how the systems are designed or applied.

Privacy is one of the most visible fault lines in this conversation. As more data is collected for social interventions, especially in humanitarian or crisis settings, questions arise about how that data is protected. Who has access to sensitive information? Are individuals aware their data being collected? Do they have a choice in the matter? In many low-resource environments, there are few legal protections, and communities may not have the technical literacy or political power to opt out or seek redress.

The ethical standards for data collection cannot be lower simply because the context is poor. If anything, they must be higher. Informed consent should be meaningful, not performative. An individual's participation should not be assumed simply because they use a service or attend a program. Privacy also goes beyond data encryption. It involves respecting the right of individuals to define how their information is used and how their identities are protected.

There is also a question of policy. Governments and institutions often lack the frameworks needed to govern data in ways that are transparent and accountable. Data governance policies, where they exist, may focus narrowly on compliance and ignore broader concerns around equity, access, and representation. In many countries, data policies are copied from high-income contexts without adapting to local legal systems, power structures, or community norms. This mismatch can create confusion and, at worst, increase harm.

Yet policy is a critical tool for shaping data systems that serve the public good. It can mandate ethical standards for data use. It can require transparency from private firms working in public spaces. It can ensure that public data is open and accessible, while protecting individuals from surveillance or misuse. For policy to work, however, it must be informed by a broad coalition technical experts, civil society, affected communities, and political leaders. It must balance innovation with protection.

Public participation in data policy is essential. People should have a voice in how data about them is collected and used. This includes not only consultation, but real influence over decision-making processes. Participatory data governance is still rare, but it is gaining momentum. Some cities have experimented with data trusts and community data councils. Others are exploring legal models that treat data as a public resource one that must be managed with care and consent.

Ultimately, the politics of data is about control. Who controls the flow of information? Who decides what is true, what is relevant, and what is fair? These are not just technical questions. They are political ones. And in the work of social good, they are central.

Data has the power to liberate, but it also has the power to exclude, to surveil, and to punish. If we fail to engage with its political dimensions, we risk building systems that reproduce the very injustices we hope to solve.

To work with data ethically, we must be willing to challenge power, protect privacy, and shape policy that reflects the values of equity and inclusion. Because data, at its best, should not just serve the powerful. It should serve the people.

Who Owns the Data?

The question of who owns the data is not just technical or administrative it's political. In the world of social impact, data is often collected from vulnerable or marginalized populations under the banner of support, development, or humanitarian aid. But once this data is gathered, who has the right to access, manage, share, or even profit from it?

In many cases, data is treated as a commodity. Governments, international agencies, non-governmental organizations, and private companies collect vast datasets about people's health, education, income, behavior, and environment. While these datasets are often justified as tools for policy and service delivery, their actual custodianship is rarely in the hands of the communities they describe. People become data subjects, but not data owners.

Ownership implies control not only over how data is stored, but how it is used. In a rural farming community, for instance, satellite and survey data might be used to map crop yields, predict pest outbreaks, or guide government subsidies. But the farmers themselves may never see the data. Worse still, the insights derived might be shared with multinational agribusiness firms before being shared with the community. This imbalance reinforces historical patterns of extraction the taking of value without reciprocal investment.

The issue becomes even more complex when data is collected by international organizations. Projects funded by donors in the Global North often extract data from communities in the Global South. These data sets are then stored in servers thousands of miles away, governed by laws those communities have no say in. In many cases, the researchers and analysts who work with the data are also far removed from the local context, which introduces layers of misunderstanding and misuse.

True data ownership would require a shift in power. Communities need the legal rights, technological infrastructure, and training to not only access their data, but to shape how it is collected, interpreted, and deployed. It means rethinking consent not as a checkbox at the beginning of a survey, but as an ongoing process. It means introducing data stewardship models where trusted local organizations act as intermediaries, ensuring that data practices align with community values and needs.

There is also the question of sovereignty. Who gets to define what data is collected in a refugee camp, an Indigenous territory, or a post-conflict zone? The absence of clear legal frameworks in many regions leaves room for exploitation. In other regions, overreaching state surveillance cloaked in development rhetoric strips citizens of privacy under the guise of progress.

Ownership isn't just about access or privacy; it's about agency. Without it, the people most affected by data-driven decisions remain voiceless in the process. And in a world increasingly shaped by algorithms and predictive systems, that voicelessness can reinforce structural injustice. The future of ethical data work must involve moving beyond inclusion toward true empowerment where communities don't just participate in data projects, they lead them.

Government Collaboration and Regulation

Governments play a central role in the data ecosystem as collectors, custodians, users, and regulators. Their collaboration can enable large-scale social good initiatives, but their involvement also raises critical questions about oversight, misuse, and power dynamics.

At their best, governments can be powerful partners in applying data to improve lives. Through national statistics offices, census bureaus, health ministries, and education departments, public institutions collect and maintain valuable datasets that inform policy and resource allocation. When governments partner with data scientists, NGOs, or private organizations with a clear public mandate, the results can be transformative. Initiatives such as open data portals, digital ID systems, and predictive tools for public health have the potential to reduce inequality, improve access to services, and drive accountability.

However, the quality of collaboration depends on context. In countries with transparent institutions and strong democratic norms, data partnerships are more likely to include public input, ethical safeguards, and legal recourse. In others, where corruption, authoritarianism, or weak institutions prevail, data can be weaponized. Surveillance of political opponents, profiling of minority groups, or data leaks that expose citizens' personal information can easily occur under the radar.

This makes regulation both necessary and difficult. Few countries in the Global South have comprehensive data protection laws equivalent to the EU's GDPR or California's CCPA. Where such laws exist, enforcement is often lax due to limited technical capacity, political interference, or lack of public awareness. In many places, digital rights are not yet seen as fundamental rights, making it difficult for citizens to demand redress when harmed by data practices.

Even when regulation is present, loopholes abound. For example, laws may protect personally identifiable information (PII) but fail to account for how anonymized data can still be re-identified. Or they may ignore how predictive analytics, and algorithmic decision-making can reinforce racial or economic discrimination even without explicit identifiers.

There's also the challenge of regulatory capture, where powerful corporate actors shape laws in ways that protect their business models over public interest. In some regions, data protection offices lack true independence from the executive branch, reducing their ability to hold governments accountable for abuses.

That said, some positive models are emerging. Countries like Kenya, Nigeria, and South Africa have taken steps to develop data privacy frameworks, although implementation remains uneven. Meanwhile, regional coalitions and civil society organizations are pushing for stronger digital rights protections and citizen-led accountability mechanisms.

Ultimately, effective government collaboration requires more than just access to public data. It demands shared values, co-designed policies, legal safeguards, and clear checks and balances. Regulators must not only understand technology, but they must also understand people. They need to be equipped not just with legal tools, but with cultural competence and community insight. Without this, well-meaning data collaborations risk enabling state overreach, undermining trust, and replicating the very inequalities they claim to address.

The goal is not to avoid government involvement but to demand better from it. For data to serve the public good, public institutions must become trustworthy stewards not extractive agents. And that trust must be earned, not assumed.

Navigating Surveillance in Humanitarian Work

Humanitarian efforts often rely on data to save lives to identify displaced populations, track disease outbreaks, allocate food and water, or monitor violence. But in the pursuit of urgency and efficiency, these well-intentioned initiatives can inadvertently create systems of surveillance. When not handled carefully, data collection in crises can turn vulnerable individuals into highly visible and permanently traceable targets.

Unlike in commercial or state settings, humanitarian contexts operate under heightened emotional, ethical, and logistical complexity. Populations affected by conflict, displacement, famine, or disaster often have little to no power to consent to data practices. Biometrics like fingerprints, iris scans, or facial recognition may be used to verify identity and deliver aid, but those same tools can be reused by authorities for tracking, detention, or exclusion. Once collected, this data rarely disappears, even when the emergency ends.

This raises urgent questions: Who else can access this information? Under what laws? And for how long? In some cases, humanitarian data systems are co-managed or later accessed by state actors, including militaries, immigration authorities, or intelligence services. When aid data becomes intelligence data, the very communities meant to be protected are placed at further risk.

The infrastructure of surveillance in these environments can be both digital and physical. From drones and mobile phone tracking to registration centers that resemble border control posts, the line between humanitarian presence and state policing can blur. Refugees, undocumented migrants, and crisis-affected populations may be monitored more intensely than any other group and they often have the least ability to refuse or contest these systems.

Even when there is no ill intent, the consequences can be devastating. A dataset shared between agencies without proper de-identification protocols can lead to mass targeting. A cloud-hosted server compromised in a cyberattack can expose thousands of records. A misapplied algorithm can flag an entire community as suspicious, delaying access to essential resources. In many humanitarian settings, the cost of surveillance isn't inconveniencing its safety, dignity, and sometimes life itself.

To navigate these risks, organizations must go beyond compliance and embrace data minimization, purpose limitation, and transparency. Data should be collected only when absolutely necessary and for specific, clearly communicated reasons. Consent must be more than a checkbox it must be contextual, informed, and revisit able. Technology choices should be informed by both technical experts and community leaders, ensuring systems reflect cultural sensitivities and lived realities.

Another solution lies in humanitarian data governance frameworks, such as the Signal Code or the Principles for Digital Development, which prioritize safety, agency, and do-no-harm. But frameworks are not enough without accountability. Humanitarian organizations must regularly audit their data practices, publish transparency reports, and involve affected populations in shaping how their data is used and protected.

In short, doing good with data cannot come at the expense of human rights. The goal of humanitarian technology should not be to see more, track more, or predict more it should be to care better. And caring better begins with restraint, reflection, and respect.

CHAPTER 9

Measuring What Matters

When data scientists speak of success, they often point to precision, recall, or accuracy, numbers that reflect how well a model performs under statistical scrutiny. But in the context of social good, success requires a broader lens. A perfectly tuned algorithm that predicts school dropouts means little if it doesn't keep children in school. A sophisticated public health dashboard may go unused if healthcare workers find it too complex. In social impact work, technical performance is not the finish line meaningful, lasting change is.

The challenge, then, is to measure what truly matters. In projects rooted in equity and human well-being, measurement must go beyond numbers. It must capture behavioral shifts, policy changes, access to rights, improved conditions, and empowered communities. It must also surface the harms, however unintended: exclusion, dependency, or surveillance. To understand whether a data initiative works, we must ask not only "Is it accurate?", but also "Is it just?", "Is it useful?", and "Is it transformative?"

In socially motivated projects, accuracy is necessary but insufficient. A tool that predicts food shortages with 90% accuracy is impressive, but does it trigger timely food distribution? Does it account for regional disparities? Does it allow for community feedback? In the pursuit of social good, impact is measured by lives improved not just models improved.

Moreover, focusing solely on accuracy may mask underlying inequities. A well-performing model might fail the very groups it was designed to serve if its training data overlooks their realities. For example, predictive policing algorithms often reinforce historical biases in law enforcement, leading to further harm under the guise of efficiency. In such cases, high accuracy can actively deepen injustice.

To evaluate real impact, practitioners must track both intended and unintended outcomes. Did behavior change? Did a community gain more agency? Did power shift in favor of those previously excluded? These are the success metrics that matter, and they often require qualitative, context-sensitive approaches.

One of the most effective tools for linking data work to social outcomes is the theory of change. It asks a basic but powerful question: "How will this project lead to the change we hope to see?" The answer isn't always linear, but mapping out the logic helps ensure that data interventions are grounded in reality.

Consider a maternal health project that aims to reduce pregnancy-related deaths. A theory of change might look like this: High maternal mortality in remote areas is the problem. The data activity is to collect geolocation and health data to map underserved regions. The output is identifying gaps in clinic coverage and emergency response times. The intermediate outcome is advocating for new health posts and mobile midwife units. And the long-term impact is safer childbirth and reduced maternal mortality.

At each stage, the theory clarifies what must happen for the data to result in change and what assumptions could break the chain. Does the data collection respect privacy? Will the health ministry act on the insights? Are there enough trained staff to deploy mobile units? These questions bring practical constraints into view early and help practitioners adjust the course before failure cascades.

Theory of change frameworks also democratize the planning process. When community members, policymakers, and data scientists co-create the model, expectations are aligned, and blind spots are reduced. It becomes a shared blueprint for what success looks like and how to measure it.

Measuring impact requires careful selection of indicators and humility in interpreting them. Too often, data projects default to what's easily countable: number of users, downloads, dashboards accessed. While these metrics are useful for monitoring activity, they rarely capture depth. A more meaningful evaluation considers indicators like whether marginalized populations gained new access to services, whether frontline workers felt more supported in their roles, whether the project led to systemic change, policy adoption, or legal reform, and whether it shifted narratives or raised awareness in ways that empowered communities.

Importantly, good metrics are not imposed from above. They are co-designed with those the project is meant to serve. A woman's cooperative in a conflict zone might define success differently than an urban policy lab. Involving communities in defining what success looks like builds trust and relevance and improves uptake.

Both quantitative and qualitative methods are vital. Numbers tell part of the story, but interviews, focus groups, and participant diaries can reveal lived experience the emotional, cultural, and relational dimensions of impact that data points miss. Qualitative feedback helps interpret what the numbers mean and whether the solution resonates with real people.

Long-term impact is often hard to measure during the project's timeline. Many interventions plant seeds that take years to bear fruit. That's why impact evaluation should not end with implementation. Instead, it should be built into the life of a project, with clear checkpoints, responsible data custodians, and accessible reporting for all stakeholders, especially the public.

Finally, practitioners must be willing to evaluate harm as well as benefit. Did the intervention cause confusion, fear, or exclusion? Did it create new burdens for already strained communities? Evaluating failure is as important as celebrating success. It is the foundation of ethical learning and sustainable improvement.

Measuring what matters is not about perfection, it is about responsibility. It calls us to shift our focus from performance metrics to people, from outputs to outcomes, and from efficiency to equity. In doing so, we unlock the true potential of data not just to predict the world as it is, but to help shape a world that is more just, inclusive, and compassionate.

Beyond Accuracy: Evaluating Social Impact

Accuracy is a comfortable benchmark in the world of data science. It provides a clear, quantifiable sense of how well a model performs within its defined parameters. But when the stakes involve human lives, fragile communities, or long-term development, accuracy becomes only one small piece of a much larger picture. In social impact work, a model can be technically impressive yet socially ineffective or even harmful. The real question is not just whether a model works, but whether it works for the people it claims to serve.

Take, for example, a health prediction algorithm that identifies regions at risk of a cholera outbreak with near-perfect precision. On paper, the results are compelling. But if the identified regions lack the infrastructure or political attention to respond, the prediction does little to change outcomes. Worse still, such data may get filed away in a report that decision-makers never read. In that case, accuracy becomes a hollow victory one that serves institutional reporting more than human wellbeing.

Evaluating social impact demands a different kind of thinking. It requires us to ask who benefits, who is excluded, and what real-world actions follow from the insights we generate. In many projects, the most critical gap is not in the model's code but in the feedback loop between insight and response. A model might accurately identify schools with high dropout rates, but does that lead to community interventions? Are the affected students and their families involved in shaping solutions? Is the root cause addressed, or is it merely labeled?

The risk of relying solely on accuracy is that it allows practitioners to feel accomplished without examining deeper consequences. For instance, predictive policing tools may achieve high arrest correlation rates, but they often rely on historically biased data, reinforcing patterns of racial profiling. Employment algorithms may reduce hiring time but filter out applicants from underrepresented groups due to subtle biases embedded in resumes or training sets. These tools are not neutral; they replicate the values, assumptions, and blind spots of the systems that produce them.

In socially complex environments, impact is often invisible to algorithms. The sense of dignity restored to a displaced family receiving aid on time. The fear experienced by a community labeled "at-risk" by a poorly communicated model. The frustration of frontline workers expected to use a data dashboard that doesn't reflect their day-to-day realities. These human experiences are often reduced to edge cases in model evaluation where the real impact lives.

True social evaluation is slow, contextual, and nuanced. It means observing how decisions evolve over time, how relationships shift, and how systems adapt. It may require ethnographic methods, qualitative interviews, and deep listening. It also means being open to uncomfortable truths: that some interventions may cause more harm than good, that others may succeed in ways we didn't predict, and that the best solutions may have nothing to do with data at all.

Ultimately, evaluating social impact means moving beyond the question "Is the model correct?" to the harder, more honest question: "What did the model do to the world once it was deployed?" In this space, success is not about clean numbers or elegant visualizations, it's about meaningful, inclusive, and measurable improvement in human lives.

Theory of Change for Data Projects

When working on data-driven interventions for social good, it's easy to become absorbed in technical tasks collecting data, cleaning it, building models, testing accuracy. But the deeper purpose of these projects lies not in code or computation, but in the transformation, they hope to support. That transformation rarely happens by accident. It requires intention, planning, and a clear sense of how each action contributes to a broader goal. This is where a theory of change becomes essential.

The theory of change is a structured way of thinking through the pathway from intervention to outcome. It lays out the logical flow of cause and effect: if we do this, then that will happen provided certain conditions are met. It connects activities like data collection or dashboard development to long-term social impacts such as improved education, reduced poverty, or increased civic engagement. Rather than assuming change will follow from good intentions, it asks for a roadmap with assumptions made explicit, stakeholders identified, and risks acknowledged.

In data science projects, a theory of change forces practitioners to step outside the technical domain and consider how their work will translate into real-world use. For example, suppose a team is building a machine learning tool to predict teacher absenteeism in rural schools. Without a theory of change, the team may stop generating accurate predictions. But with one, they begin to ask deeper questions: Will school administrators have access to the model's results? Do they have the authority to intervene? Is absenteeism rooted in factors beyond the school's control, such as unpaid salaries or poor transportation? If the answer to these questions is unclear, the entire intervention could stall not because the data is wrong, but because the pathway to action was never defined.

A strong theory of change outlines these pathways step by step. It specifies the input in this case, data about attendance and school operations and the activities, such as modeling and visualizing trends. It defines the output, such as a real-time alert system for education authorities. Then it tracks outcomes, like timely responses to absences, and ultimately, the impact: more consistent teaching and better learning outcomes for students. Each link in this chain can then be tested, monitored, and refined.

Importantly, theories of change should be built in collaboration with those who will use or be affected by the data. Community organizations, government departments, and frontline workers must be at the table. Their insights reveal whether assumptions are realistic, whether timelines are feasible, and whether the intervention truly aligns with lived experience. Without their participation, even the best-designed models risk solving problems no one has, or creating tools no one can use.

A theory of change also prepares teams for failure. By making dependencies and assumptions visible, it becomes easier to spot weak links. If a model assumes that clinics will act on predictions of malaria outbreaks, but those clinics lack medical supplies or transportation, the project must adjust perhaps by advocating for logistics support or scaling back its claims. These insights are not setbacks; they are course corrections that increase the chances of lasting impact.

At its core, the theory of change is about accountability. It demands that data scientists connect their work to human outcomes and take responsibility for the full arc of their intervention not just the part that fits on a screen. In doing so, they elevate their practice from technical execution to ethical participation in the ecosystems they seek to support. And that's where real change begins.

Indicators, Metrics, and Long-Term Outcomes

Once a data-for-good project is underway, and a theory of change has outlined the desired pathway to impact, the next challenge is measurement. It's one thing to say a project hopes to improve public health or education access but how will that improvement be tracked? What signals will indicate that real progress is being made, and what might show that something is going wrong? These questions hinge on the careful selection and interpretation of indicators, metrics, and long-term outcomes.

Indicators are not just numbers; they are stories told through data. They represent the bridge between intention and evidence. But choosing the right indicators requires deep understanding of context. Too often, projects default to what's easiest to measure: number of users, downloads, trainings completed, or times a dashboard was accessed. These outputs may signal activity, but they rarely capture whether the intervention truly benefited people or how it changed systems. A dashboard can be viewed thousands of times without influencing a single decision.

Meaningful indicators reflect what communities actually care about. For instance, in a water sanitation project, engineers might want to measure improvements in pH levels or filtration speed. But for local residents, the indicators that matter may be the number of days without diarrhea in children, the time saved walking to safe water, or the trust they have in using new purification systems. These are not abstract metrics, they are lived experiences. And without them, the project's data may miss the mark entirely.

To create relevant indicators, data practitioners must engage with local voices. Community leaders, service users, frontline workers, and even critics should be involved in identifying what success looks like and how it can be observed. This process not only improves the quality of evaluation but also builds legitimacy and trust. When people see their values reflected in the metrics, they are more likely to engage with the project and contribute to its sustainability.

Beyond the choice of indicators, the way they are measured matters. Quantitative metrics provide scope and scale they show patterns, trends, and disparities. But qualitative methods bring depth, context, and meaning. Focus groups, interviews, field notes, and observational reports can reveal how people feel, what challenges they encounter, and how their behavior changes over time. These qualitative insights make the numbers intelligible and ensure that measurement does not reduce people to data points.

Another critical aspect of measurement is the ability to track change over time. Many data-for-good initiatives are evaluated during or shortly after implementation, but their real effects may take years to emerge. A civic engagement tool might only begin to influence elections after multiple voting cycles. A gender equity dashboard may contribute to cultural shifts that unfold gradually across generations. Without long-term commitment to monitoring, such progress remains invisible, unacknowledged, and unsupported.

There is also the need to monitor unintended consequences. A system that prioritizes speed might exclude those with slower internet access. A predictive model in social services might create pressure to meet quotas rather than improve care. These outcomes may not appear in official reports, but they are part of the project's legacy. Failing to measure them can lead to repeating the same mistakes in new forms.

Ultimately, the goal of measurement in social good work is not to validate the project team's competence it is to hold the intervention accountable to the people it affects. The best metrics do not just confirm success; they challenge teams to stay humble, responsive, and ready to change course when needed. They focus not on how impressive the solution is, but on how meaningful it is to the community it claims to serve.

Measuring long-term outcomes in this way requires rigor, adaptability, and care. It demands resources for follow-up, a culture of reflection, and transparent communication of results including failures. But when done well, it provides something more valuable than data: it offers insight into what makes change real, what makes it last, and how we might do better next time.

CHAPTER 10
Building a Career or Movement in Data for Good

The idea of working in data for social goods holds deep appeal the promise of applying technical skill to real-world problems, of using algorithms not just for profit but for purpose. But turning that promise into a meaningful career or movement isn't always straightforward. This path is still emerging, shaped by individuals who are building it as they walk it, often without clear job descriptions, titles, or roadmaps to follow. The work is messy, cross-disciplinary, and sometimes undervalued but for many, it is the most fulfilling form of data science there is.

A career in data for good doesn't begin with a perfect résumé. It begins with a commitment to understanding the social context behind the code. It demands a willingness to sit with discomfort to learn about injustice, inequality, and complexity before attempting to intervene. This is not work for those chasing glamour or quick wins. It's for people who care about questions like: Who benefits from this data? Who is harmed? Who gets to decide what "good" means?

There is no single-entry point. Some people arrive through traditional paths with degrees in computer science, statistics, or public policy. Others enter from less expected routes: community organizing, journalism, education, or public health. What matters most is not where you start, but how you connect your skills to service. In this space, success is not measured by technical fluency alone, but by the ability to listen, collaborate, and remain accountable to real people not just abstract users or datasets.

Building a career in this field also means unlearning the notion of the lone genius. Social good work is not about heroic problem-solving; it is about collective impact. That means learning to work across disciplines with researchers, local leaders, legal experts, activists, and policymakers. It means sharing credit, deferring to lived experience, and accepting that sometimes the best contribution is not a solution, but a question that shifts the conversation in the right direction.

This work can be deeply rewarding, but also emotionally and mentally taxing. The problems are urgent, but the systems are slow. Change can take years, and success is often difficult to measure. Burnout is a real risk, especially when working in under-resourced settings where the need far exceeds the capacity. Sustaining a career in data for good requires boundaries, community, and a long-term perspective. It means finding peers who share your values, mentors who model humility, and spaces that allow you to recharge without guilt.

For some, this path becomes more than a career it becomes a movement. Movements don't rely on formal job titles or funding cycles. They grow from shared purpose, distributed leadership, and the courage to ask hard questions out loud. They thrive in open-source communities, civic tech meetups, local hackathons, and global networks of changemakers. Movements invite others in, especially those who've historically been excluded from technology spaces. They make knowledge public, processes transparent, and make mistakes visible so others can learn.

Storytelling plays a vital role in sustaining both careers and movements. When data practitioners share not just results but reflections on what went wrong, what surprised them, what they wish they knew they build a culture of honesty and humility. These stories serve as guideposts for others entering the field, and as reminders that behind every dataset is a human story worth respecting.

Ultimately, to build a career or movement in data for good is to choose values over convenience. It is to believe that data can be a tool for liberation, not control for justice, not just efficiency. And it is to understand that doing this work well doesn't require perfection only responsibility, curiosity, and a deep, unwavering respect for the people your work affects.

Pathways into the Field

There is no single doorway into the field of data for social good. People arrive from vastly different starting points, some through formal education in computer science or statistics, others from lived experience in communities affected by inequality, and still others from careers in journalism, health, education, or government. What they share is not a résumé template, but a mindset: the belief that data, when used ethically and intentionally, can contribute to a more just and inclusive world.

For some, the journey begins in academia. They might start by researching how algorithms affect public policy or how predictive models shape decisions in health, housing, or criminal justice. These individuals often build deep subject-matter expertise, pairing it with technical skill. Others may find their way through the nonprofit sector, joining NGOs or civil society groups where data is used to track program effectiveness, advocate for reform, or expose systemic gaps.

Increasingly, professionals from the private tech sector also pivot toward social impact roles, seeking greater alignment between their work and their values. These individuals bring with them knowledge of infrastructure, engineering, and product development but often must learn to operate in environments where the goals are not driven by profit, but by people. In such settings, success is slower, messier, and less clearly defined yet often more fulfilling.

There are also those who enter through grassroots and civic tech communities. They may not have advanced degrees, but they have built tools in response to local needs visualizing budgets, mapping environmental hazards, or creating transparency platforms. These practitioners understand the power of proximity and community insight. Their work is driven not by external metrics, but by whether their neighbors' lives improve.

Fellowships, bootcamps, and open-source initiatives have become critical bridges for people looking to enter or transition into the field. Programs focused on public interest technology, ethical AI, or humanitarian innovation provide training, mentorship, and real-world exposure. They also serve as spaces for building networks, a crucial asset in a field that often operates at the intersection of multiple disciplines.

But for all these pathways, one truth remains: this is not a space defined by credentials alone. What matters is the ability to think critically, collaborate across sectors, and remain rooted in the lived experiences of those the data represents. It is a field that rewards curiosity, humility, and the courage to speak up when systems fail or people are left out.

There are many ways to stay in and even more ways to stay in. Some will write policy, others will build tools. Some will lead institutions, others will teach, write, or organize. The important thing is not to fit into a narrow mold, but to shape your path in service of the world you want to help create.

Collaborating Across Disciplines

No data for social good project succeeds in isolation. The complexity of societal challenges from healthcare gaps and educational inequity to climate resilience and urban planning demands input from multiple domains. Technical skill alone cannot account for the cultural, political, and emotional realities that shape how people live. This is why interdisciplinary collaboration isn't just helpful in this field, it's essential.

Yet collaboration across disciplines doesn't happen by default. It takes work to bridge the languages and rhythms of different fields. A data scientist may speak in terms of variables and distributions, while a community organizer speaks in stories and histories. A policymaker might think in terms of feasibility and funding cycles, while a health worker worries about time, trust, and the trauma their patients carry. These differences can lead to friction, but they are also what make shared work more robust.

Effective collaboration starts with listening. When data professionals enter a project assuming they know the solution, they often miss the heart of the problem. Social workers, teachers, nurses, activists carry knowledge that no dataset can reveal. They know what's been tried, what's failed, what the community fears, and where its quiet strengths lie. Bringing them into the conversation early ensures that the questions being asked are the right ones and that the resulting tools reflect real needs.

Power dynamics must also be acknowledged. In many interdisciplinary teams, those with technical skills are afforded more authority even when they lack context. But if the people who understand systems are the only ones defining them, the result is often a sleek tool that no one uses. Valuing all forms of expertise, experiential, cultural, institutional is key to building trust and designing interventions that actually work on the ground.

When done well, cross-sector collaboration can be transformative. It leads to tools that are not just functional but intuitive, not just scalable but sensitive. A predictive model built with teachers may be simpler, but it's more likely to be used. A public dashboard designed with community groups may have fewer features, but it will reflect their values and voice.

It also makes the work more sustainable. When stakeholders co-create a solution, they're more likely to advocate for it, fund it, and integrate it into their existing systems. Instead of an external project that needs constant support, the intervention becomes part of the community's own toolkit for change.

Collaboration also allows for better reflection. In data science, there can be pressure to perform to build fast, publish early, impress funders. But in a multidisciplinary team, there's more room to ask: "Should we be doing this at all?" "What harm might come from this tool?" "What don't we know yet?" These questions slow down the rush to solve, and they often lead to stronger, more thoughtful outcomes.

Ultimately, collaborating across disciplines is an act of humility. It's the willingness to recognize that no one person, team, or field has all the answers. It's a commitment to building solutions not for communities, but with them and to letting those closest to the problem help shape the path forward. In the space of social good, this is not just good practice, it's the only path that leads to meaningful, lasting change.

Sustaining Impact Through Community and Storytelling

Doing meaningful work in data for social good is not just about launching tools or analyzing trends, it's about staying the course. The real impact of this work is often slow, subtle, and cumulative. A model may take months to build, but the social change it seeks might unfold over years, across generations, and through our hands we may never meet. To sustain that kind of impact, data professionals must move beyond individual projects and toward community not just as a user group, but as a source of energy, feedback, and accountability.

The nature of this work can be isolating. Practitioners often operate at the edges of multiple systems technology, government, nonprofit, and academia without fully belonging to any. In these margins, it's easy to burn out, especially when resources are scarce and the stakes are high. But a community of peers, mentors, and co-conspirators can provide the support necessary to keep going. Communities offer more than camaraderie they provide perspective. They remind us that failures are not final, that ethical dilemmas are shared, and that the work is not ours alone to carry.

Building community also means investing in local knowledge. Too often, data-for-good projects are driven by external actors who disappear once funding ends. But when communities are part of the design, leadership, and evaluation, they become stewards of the project's evolution. What starts as an intervention becomes infrastructure sustained not by outside attention, but by local relevance and ownership. This shift from dependency to agency is the true measure of success.

Alongside community, storytelling is the thread that binds intention to impact. Data may guide decisions, but stories move people. They translate numbers into meaning, models into memory, and insights into action. A chart might show declining dropout rates, but a student's voice explaining how a data-informed policy changed their life will move policymakers faster than a dataset ever could.

Yet in the world of data science, storytelling is often underused or misunderstood. It's not about branding or polishing the truth, it's about communicating complexity with honesty. Sharing how a project was built, what it struggled with, where it failed, and who it helped (or didn't) builds trust. It encourages reflection and invites others to contribute, critique, or carry the work forward in new directions.

Storytelling is also a form of resistance. In spaces where data is used to erase people to reduce them to risk scores or probabilities a story reclaims their humanity. It reminds us that behind every data point is a person with history, context, and agency. And in doing so, it keeps the work grounded in its highest purpose: not just to see the world more clearly, but to change it more justly.

To sustain impact, practitioners must document their journeys, amplify community voices, and build ecosystems where knowledge is shared, not siloed. This work is not about one big breakthrough, but about many small contributions that, together, shape a more equitable future. The tools will change. The technology will evolve. But what will endure are the relationships, the trust, and the stories told and retold that carry the work across time and space.

www.ingramcontent.com/pod-product-compliance
Lightning Source LLC
LaVergne TN
LVHW092008090526
838202LV00001B/45